WE NEVER WALK ALONE

V. Ray Camp

Copyright © 2006 by V. Ray Camp

We Never Walk Alone
by V. Ray Camp

Printed in the United States of America

ISBN 1-59781-855-0

All rights reserved solely by the author. The author guarantees all contents are original and do not infringe upon the legal rights of any other person or work. No part of this book may be reproduced in any form without the permission of the author. The views expressed in this book are not necessarily those of the publisher.

Unless otherwise indicated, Bible quotations are taken from King James Version. Copyright © 1994 by Zondervan Publishing House.

www.xulonpress.com

CONTENTS

TESTIMONY I 15
TESTIMONY II 21
TESTIMONY III 25
TESTIMONY IV 31
TESTIMONY V 39
TESTIMONY VI 43
TESTIMONY VII 51
TESTIMONY VIII 57
TESTIMONY IX 65
TESTIMONY X 71
TESTIMONY XI 79
TESTIMONY XII 83
EPILOGUE 107

ACKNOWLEDGMENTS

I thank my Lord, Jesus Christ, for giving me the greatest gift I could ever want or need—His promise of eternal life in heaven to dwell with Him forever.

I also give my Lord all the glory and honor, because it is by my Lord's love and mercy that I was blessed with an ability I can use to serve Him, and because He inspired me to write something that will serve Him for a long time and help other people come to Him and be saved.

I cannot begin to thank all the folks who were so gracious in granting me an interview so I could have the blessing of hearing each testimony firsthand. My blessings from this experience alone are immeasurable to me.

I especially thank my Lord, Jesus, for placing Pastor Scott Willis before me as my shepherd who led me to Jesus and was so very kind and patient with me in those first years after my salvation.

PREFACE

I became a Christian in 1985 and since then have taken notice of God's hand in my life. One day it occurred to me that God must have had His hand on my life for a long, long time. In fact, I began to theorize that He was with me from the moment I was conceived in my mother's womb. Now, I thought, if this is true for me, then it must be true for everyone on earth. The more I reflected on my life, the more I became convinced that God is with me now and has always been with me.

I discovered that God was calling me to come to know His forgiveness by accepting Jesus, His Son, as my Savior from the moment of my conception until I accepted Jesus. After that, He was more than just with me; He was in me and walking with me every step I took. When I experienced trouble and strife, I knew it was Him carrying me through that I was able to successfully negotiate those experiences.

Now, for longer than I can remember, I have been asking God to give me something I can do to serve Him and I felt that I was never receiving an answer. That was because I wasn't paying attention. My mission was constantly before my eyes and I did not recognize it. You see, I have been writing since my young teen years. I have written fiction, poetry, and recently my memoirs. God has given me the talent to write. I know I may never be a great and well-known writer, but I am not doing this for fame or fortune, although I would have to admit I would have difficulty turning either away. I am, after all, only human. No, I am writing this book because this is what my Lord wants me to do. He wants me to tell the world that He is and has always been with each of us and will continue until the moment of our death. At that moment He will stop calling to you and will judge you accordingly. If you reject Jesus, then upon your death you will be forever apart from God. I am inspired by God to write this so you can be shown that you need salvation more than you need anything else on earth and you need God because He is the Almighty and His Son Jesus is the light and the way. You cannot come to the Father except that you come to Him through Jesus Christ, the Son of God and the Savior of all mankind.

> For God so loved the world, that he gave his only begotten Son, that whosoever believeth in him should not perish, but have everlasting life. For God sent not his Son into the world to condemn the world; but that the world through him might be saved.
>
> John 3:16-17

God knows every single person on earth from the moment of their conception until the moment of their physical death. God works in everyone's life every single moment to try to draw each one to Him.

When something happens to you, God uses it to try to draw you to Him. He wants you to call on Him for your needs, to depend on Him for your needs, and to lay those needs at His feet. God does not cause the things that happen on this earth; however, He does allow all that happens, because of sin on the earth. So when you find yourself in any kind of trouble, He is waiting to answer your prayers. All you need do is to pray.

When you pray to God for help, you are asking Him to change something or make it better. He will always answer your prayer. He will not always answer it the way you expect. He will answer your prayer according to His will, which almost always is different from yours.

Everyone who has prayed to God more than once will tell you that things are not always made better, at least according to their perspective. God answers all of our prayers; from those who call themselves Christians to those who claim to be atheists. The answer He decides upon is often tied to who is doing the asking.

When a lost soul finally prays to God out of desperation, the answer that person receives is what God has decided will best draw that person to Him. Oftentimes, it is not the answer the person was looking for when they prayed. When a Christian prays, that person is usually asking for God's intervention in something. God's answer is not always yes. I once knew of a person who had lymph cancer and she died despite a multitude of prayers. God brought her to Him and she accepted Jesus before she died. God did make it better for her. She now has eternal life and is in heaven with our Lord. She accepted Jesus as her Savior before her death and that was prayers answered. That woman was my step-mother, Stephanie.

God wants all people to come to know Him and to spend eternity with Him in heaven. This is why God is with each of us every moment of our life. He wants us to repent of our sins, accept His Son, Jesus Christ as our Savior and become born again. He has called all of us to this end, but few will be chosen. It is because we choose not to accept God's offer of salvation and therefore never become reborn into the family of God.

> Whosoever believeth that Jesus is the Christ is born of God: and every one that loveth him that begat loveth him also that is begotten of him. By this we know that we love the children of God, when we love God, and keep his commandments. For this is the love of God, that we keep his commandments: and his commandments are not grievous. For whatsoever is born of God overcometh the world; and this is the victory that overcometh the world, even our faith. Who is he that overcometh the world, but he that believeth that Jesus is the Son of God? This is he that came by water and blood, even Jesus Christ; not by water only, but by water and blood. And it is the Spirit that beareth witness, because the Spirit is truth.
>
> 1 John 5:1-6

I have gathered some testimonies from folks just like you and me. These stories show how the Lord works in our lives to call us to Him.

Our Lord is always with you from the moment of your conception until the moment of your death. Upon your death you must face Him for your final judgment. You will either be accepted into heaven with God forever or you will be forever apart from Him. The following testimonies show that God wants you to be with Him in heaven and that He calls to you every moment of your life. You have the opportunity to be born again in Christ. Once you accept Him as your Savior, you have God's promise of eternal life with Him in heaven.

An atheist and a Christian are both sinners. One is no better than the other. The only thing a Christian has that an atheist does not have is that a Christian has forgiveness of his sins by the grace of God through the blood of Jesus Christ. An atheist has no forgiveness and no hope of eternal life with God. After all, according to the atheist, God does not exist.

Reading this book will help you to understand the promise that the Lord made to His own—that He would always be with us and as those who have accepted Him as our Savior—we know we will never walk alone because He is with us, in our good times and during our various crises.

A detailed blueprint or road map to salvation is provided in the last pages for your personal benefit. It is my deepest desire that you will decide this message is directed at you, that you will accept Jesus as your Savior, and be born again to begin the first day of the rest of your life knowing His grace, mercy, and love.

> The Lord is my shepherd; I shall not want. He maketh me to lie down in green pastures: He leadeth me beside the still waters. He restoreth my soul: He leadeth me in the paths of righteousness for his name's sake. Yea, though I walk through the valley of the shadow of death, I will fear no evil: for thou art with me; thy rod and thy staff they comfort me. Thou preparest a table before me in the presence of my enemies: thou annointest my head with oil; my

cup runneth over. Surely goodness and mercy shall follow me all the days of my life: and I will dwell in the house of the Lord forever.

Psalm 23

There is a family of loving, caring people today who, by a single common bond, enjoy a life that is full in all the things that really matter, rich in all the things that really matter, and joyful in all the things that really matter. Although membership in this family is open to all who desire it, and all members are adopted (no one is born into it), there is a single requirement you must fulfill before you join: you must accept Jesus Christ, the Son of God and the Savior of man, as personal Savior. This done, you will gain membership as a child of the family of God. The children of the family of God are known as Christians and Christians are followers of Christ.

The benefits of being a child of God are that your sins—past, present, and future—are forgiven by God. You will enter into a covenant with Him that you will no longer be condemned to death but you will have everlasting life with Him in heaven. Your rewards and joy are beyond earthly description.

Every day of our lives we make decisions and if we have faith that the Lord will not allow us to follow through on a bad decision, so long as we follow His direction, then we also have assurance that, whatever the outcome, it will be what He wants for us. There are times when we like the results and there are times we do not, but we know all things come to good for those who love the Lord.

These are the testimonies of our lives, each one of us being a part of the body of Christ. Each person in this book has offered testimony of their salvation, which is the way each came to know Christ as Savior. Each has also included their story that shows we will never walk alone because He will always be with us.

****

TESTIMONY I

Sue Mezykowski has testimony of her journey to come to know the Lord and of the Lord's hand working not only in her life, but also in the lives of her family.

The Lord used friends and her youngest daughter to bring her to Him. Later in life, it was her faith and prayer that drew her other child and that child's husband into the family of God. Sue's husband, Dave, was eventually saved and the family's prayers for her eldest daughter's husband, Joe, were answered by God in a very miraculous way.

My story about how I got saved goes back to the early 80's. Some friends of ours, Rainier and Theresa Hyena, had taken our little girl, Angela to their church. They had been saved a couple of years before and were attending the Faith Temple, which is on Elsner Road in Frankfort, Illinois. They always took their little girls to a Sunday night children's ministry called Missionettes and they had asked our little Angela if she would like to go. I had given my permission, so they took her and she really enjoyed it. We could see there was a noticeable change in Angela. Our painfully shy little girl had become quite joyful and there was a difference in her that was almost indescribable.

Angela's teachers had always said she was a good little girl, but wouldn't talk to them. They said she did good paperwork, but they could never get her to raise her hand in class. Then suddenly, this little girl who had been so introverted and shy had become outgoing and different. We were quite joyful and knew it related to her going to that Sunday night children's ministry. Dave and I, being the parents we are, wanted to delve into what was going on there. We wanted to find out what was changing her and what was making her look forward to being with these people and being so happy. We soon found out what it was. She had become saved and that was what had made her different. She was emerging as a new little creation who was joyful and who knew the Lord long before we did.

One day, Dave and I were invited to a Sunday evening service at that church and we decided to go just go once and that would be it. We would find out what was going on and make sure our child was involved in something that was OK. However, once we went, well we just never stopped going. I guess the Lord captured us. Only a few months later, one Sunday morning, I gave my heart to the Lord and I praise God because my husband followed several months later.

The picture that was drawn for me by a very dear friend and which made me want to know Jesus more was that when we come before the Lord at that last judgment and when God looks down upon us, Jesus is going to be there with His arms around us saying, "Father, this is one of Mine."

I wanted that for me. I wanted to be with Jesus and hear Him proclaiming me as His. I thank God He did that for us.

Actually, what makes me know the differences in my life is that the weight of sin no longer has power over me. I know I have been forgiven. I know the joy that has been lifted.

I know that on one particular Sunday morning, I cannot tell you exactly which one, I was compelled to go forward and give my heart to the Lord. Nothing could have kept me in my seat. Only a few months later, after Dave had accepted the Lord, we were baptized together to proclaim our belief in Jesus.

Since then, the Lord has been not only with me, but with my entire family. This has proven true, especially through this past year.

I am not sure how many know most of the details about my son-in-law, Joe, and what went on in the last year or so. God has been so good and so faithful through that whole situation.

Joe was diagnosed with mitro valve regurgitation and had undergone one operation that repaired the valve by putting a ring in to prevent the leakage in his heart. Within a month, without anyone knowing it, an infection had gotten into the heart. He began having strokes. They finally realized this man was going to die because of this infection. They had to remove the ring they had placed in his heart. This meant a second open heart surgery; a second time to crack his chest open; a second time for him to experience the pain he had gone through before. None of us will ever know what that felt like except Joe. He's a dear guy—a brave guy. But how brave can you be when you think of someone having to slice you open once again and saw through your sternum again, and open your chest once again, and open your heart once again? How scary is that? So his wife, who is also my daughter, knew the fear he was probably facing with that second heart operation the next morning.

They had said, "You are a ticking time bomb, Joe. We have to do this. We have to take out the ring the infection has attached itself to."

We left him that night, knowing what he was facing in the morning. We stayed at the hospital. The hospital has rooms for close relatives of a patient who is very sick. They are like hotel rooms and we were blessed to get one that night.

Linda and I were both scared to be facing Joe the next morning. We were scared we were going to face a man who was himself scared, because he knew what was coming. We prayed before we fell asleep, not that there was much sleep that night. The hardest part I was facing, I thought, was walking back into that hospital room the next morning to see Joe before the surgery. I dreaded facing him. I dreaded seeing the look of fear. I dreaded feeling frightened for him of what was coming. But I forgot one thing. I forgot what an awesome God we serve. I forgot the power of that God that we serve.

That morning, Linda and I walked slowly to that room and as we turned the corner, we saw Joe. You could cut the peace in that room with a knife.

Joe looked up and smiled and said, "I prayed all night and I'm okay. This is going to be okay. I'm going to get through this. I prayed all night and I know God is going to be with us."

I just thank God so much for that gift. That was such a gift that morning to walk into that room and to feel the presence of God and know that God had given Joe such peace and in turn, us as well. What a gift that was—to see and feel the peace in that room. Facing possible death; facing so much pain; God had wrapped His arms around Joe and he was at peace. So much at peace that several people came to visit and we could all feel it; we could all sense it. Joe was at peace.

His surgery was not until one o'clock that afternoon but he was so at peace he even fell asleep about an hour before the surgery. He fell asleep and napped while we stood in the room and prayed. Only my God could have handled that in that way and I thank You, Lord, for that gift. I will never forget that — the peace that passes all understanding. I appreciate it so much.

The second surgery was a success; they were able to remove the ring in Joe's heart and flush out some of the infection. This was followed by several months of intravenous antibiotics (the strongest ones known to man), administered under home care. His wife, having learned how to administer the antibiotics, became very proficient at the task, which was given through a tube inserted in his chest.

A couple of months after the antibiotics were done; another test was performed to check the status of Joe's heart. After the test, the cardiologist walked into the room and declared, "Joe's heart is normal! There is no sign of leakage and scar tissue has formed over the original repair and is now holding the original repair in place. He may never need a third operation to replace the ring on the valve."

In essence, God restored Joe's heart. Hallelujah!

When we go through trials and turmoil, we often wonder, "Why Lord? What are You trying to teach us? Where are You taking us with this?" I think what I've learned in this past year is that we serve a God of behavior modification. If we're going down one path and He wants us to go down a different path, He is going to find a way to try to help us down that different path, and sometimes He does it in ways that are very hard, but it has a way of getting us to where He wants us to be.

Joe and Linda now have drastically changed lives; have but praise God; I feel they have understood where God wants them to be. They have been blessed that Joe has been able to get Social Security disability. That is a blessing in itself. Now they are both going full time to college, hoping to get degrees as registered nurses. The plan is that when the children are grown they can take this to a mission field. They would never have thought of doing this a year ago, that

God could turn this all around and somehow use it to further the kingdom.

We are so blessed they realize God has a plan in their lives. And we are grateful, also, that Joe was able to get his high school diploma. That's been part of the blessing as well.

Through all of this, Joe and Linda saw the need for compassionate people in the medical field. They had all kinds of people taking care of them; those who were the most compassionate seemed to also give the best care and that is where they would like to be some day.

****

TESTIMONY II

Many people come to know Christ by faith, yet there are always a few who cannot believe unless they can see it, or touch it, or smell it. The Bible tells us of Thomas, called Didymus, one of the twelve apostles who was not with them when Jesus was resurrected and was told by them some days later. Thomas did not believe them and said, "Except I shall see in his hands the print of the nails, and put my finger into the print of the nails, and thrust my hand into his side, I will not believe."

John 20:25

And after eight days again his disciples were within, and Thomas with them: then came Jesus, the doors being shut, and stood in the midst, and said, Peace be unto you. Then saith he to Thomas, Reach hither thy finger, and behold my hands; and reach hither thy hand, and thrust it into my side: and be not faithless, but believing. And Thomas answered and said unto him, my Lord and my God. Jesus saith unto him, Thomas, because thou hast seen me, thou hast believed: blessed are they that have not seen, and yet have believed.

John 20:26-29

Thomas did not have the faith to believe and needed proof of Jesus' resurrection and the Lord offered him his proof. Our Lord did not punish Thomas or smite him with disease or pestilence, Jesus merely showed Thomas the wounds from His crucifixion and Thomas believed.

Also, in Judges 6, a man named Gideon had an argument with God. God told him things that would occur and Gideon kept asking God how it could happen, but God patiently answered. God knew, then as He knows now, that we always doubt Him and He patiently guides us in spite of ourselves.

Dave Mezykowski is somewhat like a Thomas or a Gideon and gives this testimony about how he became saved and how the Lord worked in his life at the same time.

I think my testimony is kind of in two pieces. This goes back to how I was saved in 1986. We were saved because God touched our daughter first.

Angela was going to church, Faith Temple in Frankfort, and going to their Daisy program for little girls. She was so happy when she was there; this was very different from our church experience prior to that. We were invited and we went to the church. Angela was saved, Sue was saved, but I wasn't. I tend to be someone who is kind of ... well, I think of myself as Mr. Scientific. I need a reason for everything.

A couple of months later, this would be in June of 1986, we were going to the church. I wasn't saved yet, and I went out into the garage and we had this old, big, heavy wooden garage door that was connected to wheels, attached to springs, and it was very clunky. I went in there to do something and so I was going to back out the car. As I stood in there, I started to push the garage door up by hand. It started to slip. I was trying to fix it and I realized this heavy wooden door was coming down and I knew I could not hold it up. I prayed, "God, help me please, I can't do this alone."

Like Gideon, I guess I needed proof and God gave it to me. He did not have to but He proved Himself to me.

I was looking for my proof, I guess, and this is how the Lord proved Himself. I was able to hold up that weight with one hand while I pushed those wheels, which had gotten out of the track, back in place. I don't know how much that weighs, but I'm sure it weighed more than thirty or forty pounds. That, I guess, was my proof; I realized there is no way I could do that myself.

I went to church that night and I told the Lord that He had proved Himself to me and I know now that I am truly saved. I made Him prove Himself and He did it. He has proved Himself so many times since.

The person who talked to you prior to me was my wife and she talked about my son-in-law, Joe. I've been saying all along, and this goes back maybe sixteen years, that I have faith. I've been saying all along that Joe, who had the surgery, that God would heal his heart. He has been back to the doctor since all those surgeries. Joe's heart is normal, which means it has healed beyond where it was before he had his first surgery. The scar tissue has taken the place of the ring and it is stronger than the repair ring ever was. He has proven Himself to me so many times. How can I ever doubt Him again?

****

TESTIMONY III

Robert Morlan is the founder of Grace Fellowship Church and has remained the pastor since its inception on March 3, 1993. His story of salvation and the Lord's hand in his life is one that deserves to be told—and retold. He has related numerous stories, testifying that he never walks alone. I only regret that I could not persuade him to tell all of them at this one interview.

The Lord was working in the Morlan's lives even before Pastor knew the Lord. His story not only tells about his salvation, but also testifies that our Lord is always with us and we need never walk alone so long as we know Jesus as our Lord and Savior.

You asked me to begin by sharing about how I came to know the Lord. I'm not sure when it all started. Who knows when the Lord really begins dealing with you, because you're not sensitive to those things? In retrospect, you see a lot of things in your life that you might think was God ordered; however, it seems as if God puts things in our way that brings us to a certain point.

I remember that I became an atheist as a result of my parents getting divorced. I was very angry with my father. I can remember one night when I was in Alaska lying in my bunk. I was in the army. This was in 1965. I remember that I was praying, because I tried to say a little prayer every night before I went to sleep, and this night I just kind of threw my hands up and said, "That's it. I'm not going to pray any more. I don't believe that You exist. I don't know why I even bother!"

That really did begin a time I didn't believe God existed. That went on for several years.

After Jann and I had been married for several years, it turned out that Jann had a problem with carrying children to term. She carried two babies to eight months and they both died.

Then we had the opportunity to adopt and I remember that I was desperate, because there was a chance we weren't going to get this baby we were planning on for six months. We had the room ready and everything else, and my wife was all excited.

At this point she was already in a pretty bad emotional state from losing the two babies. I remember the lawyer called and told us we had a boy. We were all excited. Twenty-four hours later he called back and said that there was a pretty good possibility that this woman was going to change her mind. As I look back, I could see that God had me in a box. I didn't have any place to turn.

I couldn't depend on my own resources, because I couldn't go and talk to the girl. There was absolutely nothing on this earth I could do about this situation. God had me right where He wanted me. Finally, I remember the day that I stood in my office and said, "I don't believe You exist."

That sounds crazy; talking to a God you don't believe exists. I said, "I'll tell You what. I don't care whether You exist or not. Personally, that's not even the issue, but if You will let us have this child, I promise I will take him to church and I will let him determine whether You exist or not."

I felt stupid saying that. I really did. I mean, I'm talking to a God I don't believe in.

We got the baby and I remember it was about nine months later that I remembered I had made a promise. I thought, if God *does* exist, He's so mean and so cruel and so vindictive that He'll take this child from us. And besides that, I had made a promise. It was a matter of my word saying I would do something.

We started going to this Baptist church. Four years later we were saved. I remember the night I was saved, I called up this Baptist pastor and asked him to come over to my house at about two or three o'clock in the morning. I told him I had been an atheist.

About a year and a half before this I had fallen in a lake up in Canada. It was not a life-threatening situation. I came out onto the shore of the lake and I was looking around at the beautiful islands, the lake, and the trees and all that stuff and I felt surely that there must be something that created all of this.

Romans chapter 1 says God reveals Himself through nature. That is how God started to reveal Himself to me.

I said to God, "If You exist, You need to show me. I want some hard evidence. I'm not going to believe unless I see."

A year and a half later, on January 17, 1976, God came calling. There was somewhat of a struggle with it. Finally, after a couple of hours I spent with this preacher, I was able to bow my head and pray for the first time that Christ would be my Lord and Savior.

Obviously, that was the greatest event in my life. I can remember it as if it happened yesterday. I can tell you, almost detail for detail, how everything went that night.

This is getting to the heart of the conversation we are having about how you know that God is with you. How do we know that when we make a decision or we are on a journey that God has not only ordered it, but that He is there with us?

About six months after I became a Christian, I could sense that the Lord was calling me to be a preacher. That was the last thing in the world I wanted. He could have asked me to be a coal miner quicker than He could have a preacher. I didn't want any part of being a preacher. Finally, after about six more months of struggle, I said, "OK Lord, I'll do it."

We sold everything and left here; Jann, my two children John and Susan and me. John was probably in the first grade and Susan was in the third grade. We moved out of this nice big home and into a home in southern Missouri—we could actually buy a house down there cheaper than we could rent. We had a few dollars left from the sale of our house and we put it down. Our house payment was $105 a month.

Jann and I started school together in September of 1978 and soon realized that both of us couldn't go to school. She had to quit and get a job. In retrospect, if I were confronted with that again I would have had her not quit. I would have said God would provide for us.

I think it is equally important for the pastor's wife to be educated as it is for the pastor.

So we were in southern Missouri; I a full-time student, and we didn't have any money. Jann got a job at a school for $525 a month. It was money provided by the government because the school district was very poor. In fact, we lived in the poorest county in Missouri and certainly didn't do anything to raise the level of poverty when we moved into town.

We spent from eighty to a hundred dollars a month on gas, because she traveled thirty miles each way to work. That left us with a little over four hundred dollars a month for our house payment, a car payment, and my tuition of $7,200 a year. I don't recall if that included books. We also paid about eighty dollars a month to heat our house in the winter and about eighty dollars a month to cool it in the summer. That left us with a little over three hundred dollars a month to pay our utilities, insurance, food, tuition, and clothing. Actually, it was more than that, because I went through summer school as well, and had to pay so much an hour. The incredible thing about it was that it probably was one of the best times ever in our lives. That was probably the greatest faith builder Jann and I ever had.

We were new Christians and didn't understand a lot. We did know that God had sent us there. There was no question in either of our minds about that. We didn't know much about Scripture, but we did know that God will take care of us if we are obedient to Him.

We knew God had come along beside us. We knew He was there providing for us.

I remember one day sitting in the student union and talking to some other pastors. There were quite a few who were older guys like me. I was in my thirties. One pastor had two or three children and said something about getting food stamps and getting free lunches. He asked me if I was doing that and I said, "No I'm not, and furthermore, I'm not going to." I told him I thought it was a sin for him to do it. He was offended. I refused to take that and commented to him and the other pastors that God had called me down here and He had promised me that if I did, He would provide for our needs. Every one of our needs He would take care of. I said that if I had to depend on the government to feed my children at school and if I had to depend on the government for food stamps so I could put food on my table, then I'm out of here because I had misread God.

That fellow is no longer in the ministry; I read about him in our school paper about a year ago.

I didn't work while I was there. I worked on the house we had bought and when we left there, two-and-a-half years later, I owed thirteen hundred dollars on my tuition. We sold our house and made about thirteen thousand dollars. We bought it for thirteen thousand and sold it for twenty-six thousand. We left with about ten or twelve thousand more than we had when we arrived, plus I had my college education paid for.

This was probably the defining moment in my Christian faith in terms of knowing how God provides when He calls us to do something. The Bible teaches us that God says, "Lo, I am with you always even unto the end of the earth" (Matthew 28:20).

I have always been able to go back and look at that time when God provided; to this day I don't know how we did it. We only had two hundred and fifty dollars a month and two children and the expense of them being in school. Yet, we prospered. There was never a time we didn't have food. There was one time when we couldn't buy a gallon of milk. It cost about a dollar, I think. We didn't have a dollar, but that only lasted for a couple of hours. God just miraculously provided.

It's during those times in life that God not only prepares us for something bigger, but He also builds our faith. We literally learn the Scripture that He will provide for us, no matter what the need. That is probably the greatest single event that has ever happened to me in my life as a Christian, in terms of knowing that God is there; God is taking care; God is providing.

****

TESTIMONY IV

Scott Kircher, one of our newest associate pastors, came to Grace Fellowship Church in 1997 from another church. He had been a Christian for some five years and after a little over a year and a half of membership at GFC, was appointed and confirmed by the congregation as a deacon in January of 1999.

By October of 2000, he began to feel the call to pastor. God had a plan for Scott. He began to implement His plan long before the year 2000.

I was raised in a not very religious home. We would go to church occasionally; once a month, sometimes more.

After I got married and Laura became pregnant with our first child, we knew we wanted to bring up our child in some sort of faith program. Being a non-Christian at the time, I really didn't care what that was. I had a background in Catholicism and intellectually believed those things, but I had some problems with what I thought was hypocrisy in my own experiences with that church. So we decided to find a church we could go to together. My wife wasn't Catholic and we decided we were going to try to find a non-denominational church.

I might have said at that time I was a Christian, but looking back I know I was not. I had some intellectual knowledge, but no saving faith. What I wanted was something like the Catholic Church, where I could go in on Sunday, and leave and remain anonymous, but hear a good message and feel better about myself. God, however, had other plans.

We started attending a church. Laura was pregnant with Jason. We wanted to bring up our child in some sort of religious faith, so we began attending a non-denominational church and I praise the Lord that it was a Bible-believing, Bible-teaching church. It was there I really heard and understood, for the first time, what the gospel was and what it meant to my life—that Jesus Christ died for my sins, that the things I had done had separated me from God and that it was only through Jesus that I could come, accept Him, and gain a righteousness that was not my own, but His and He would take away the sins I had committed because He died for them.

After realizing that and being in the church for several months, I came to a point in early 1993 of true belief and understanding of what Christ had done; I accepted Him as my Savior.

At the time of my conversion, I did not have a big emotional experience. I am not a very emotional person, so it was more of a logical understanding of what Christ had done for me. My acceptance was really an act of my will, and it certainly affected my intellect and my emotions, but not to the extent of some people.

As I continued in my new-found walk with Christ, I began by crawling. I was doing Bible study in a men's group. I began turning over areas of my life as the Spirit within started seeping out of me as I grew; turning over finances, possessions, and letting Christ take over those things. As I look back, I can see there was one thing I wanted to keep—control of my family. I certainly loved them and could provide for them better than anyone else—even God. I thought I loved them more than even God loved them at that time.

This went on for maybe a year and a half, maybe closing in on two years. Then Laura became pregnant with our second child and when he was born, Adam had some difficulty breathing on his own. They had put him on oxygen and later had to put him on a respirator because his blood wouldn't oxygenate. He was just gasping and trying, for the first twenty-four hours, to breath on his own but he couldn't. As the first few days wore on, it was very difficult for us. Laura had to come home from the hospital. It was difficult to leave our child there in the hospital. Coming home without our baby was really hard. I remember that throughout that time people were praying for Adam and for us. Laura and I were praying for Adam and that he would be healed.

During the first week, being home without him, going there every day and getting reports from the doctors, it was apparent they didn't understand why his blood wasn't oxygenating completely. They didn't know why there was fluid in his lungs and they were performing many tests.

They had to keep turning up the pressure on his respirator; they could only turn it up just so high, because it would cause damage in the blood vessels in the brain. I remember getting a call from the doctor about eight days after Adam was born, saying they couldn't turn up the pressure any higher and would have to move him to a jet respirator.

Laura was a respiratory therapist. I remember getting off the phone with the doctor and talking to her. She said that was a kind of last resort when they don't know what else to do. At least this was true at the hospital she worked at during this time. Many times the babies died.

I remember getting into the shower right after that and just crying my eyes out, crying out to God. It was really there that I felt God impress upon me as if saying, *"You know, you trust Me with things that are not eternally important; money; your possessions—those type of things. Yet you don't trust Me with the things that are eternally important—your family's lives."*

At that point I totally gave everything to God. This is the place that I was absolutely affected in my emotions and in every part of my being.

I remember saying to God, "You know what? I know You love me. You sent Your own Son to die for me. I know You love my family even more than I do and if You choose to call Adam home right now, I accept that and I am going to trust You with him."

At that point I really was prepared and I really thought Adam was going to die, that he wasn't going to come home.

Certainly, things in my life would have changed if he had died. He didn't. He ended up coming home two days later. He was off the respirator and completely fine.

That was not a testimony to my submission or anything else, but a testimony to the grace of God and how He wants to bless us. And it was through that time that my spiritual growth, instead of just kind of going slowly, really took off.

I don't think that any of that would have changed had Adam died, or where I would be today if he would have died, because I was absolutely prepared for his death. I really thought he would. God is so graceful and so merciful to us and He desires to bless us so much that He healed Adam and he came home. I praise the Lord he is with us today and is as healthy as anyone.

Turning over those areas of life helped me to really understand how loving God is. How God desires us to just trust in Him with every segment of our life—every part of it—because that is when we really find peace and joy and happiness. When we hold things back, we miss out on some of the things God wants us to experience and the closeness He wants us to have with Him in a relationship with Him.

Despite the difficult circumstances and the hard times that Laura and I went through, I wouldn't give that time away for anything in the world. I wouldn't desire to go through it again, but I know what God did to both me and Laura through that time. That time was really formative in the shaping of who I am today, of what God has done in my life, how He has grown me over the years. That is the time I always look back to as one of the turning points or platforms for my growth that, if I hadn't gone through, I wouldn't be where I am today.

I felt God was with me the whole time and had not abandoned me, but I don't think I really understood what He was trying to teach me or what He was trying to do. Not until I got into that shower and cried out to God and just sensed Him asking me that question, *"Are you really trusting in Me completely with everything? I want so much more for you."*

He was there for me throughout the whole thing. It was really a point of me fully giving over my entire life and dropping to my knees before the Lord saying, "I am completely Yours in everything."

I can't explain what happened. Nothing was done differently. Jordan just began to start oxygenating and they ended up being able to take him off the respirator. We went to the hospital one day, I don't remember if it was the next day or the day after that, but when we went in he was off the respirator and breathing on his own.

God is certainly with us and I see in my own life that God is with us and wants to bless us. But at the same time, I know there are many faithful Christians whose children have died. I wouldn't, for even one minute, say that it was because they didn't learn or because they didn't do what they were supposed to do. Adam's well-being did not have anything to do with my obedience or anything. I don't believe that. I believe it has everything to do with the grace and mercy of God. Certainly, through that time, God did want to bring me to my knees and did want me to come before Him and He did place me in a position where I did have the option to acknowledge Him as Lord of everything, not just of things that do not really matter. We do put a lot of importance on money and possessions, but when we stop and think about it, when we can trust God with the things that have eternal consequences—our family's lives have eternal consequences—that produces in us the opportunity to move closer to God and know that closer relationship. That is what God desires in all of us. He will do what He has to do to put us in a position so we can acknowledge Him and we can grow closer to Him. God is fully in control of the circumstances of life. He is fully in control of all things. If I had not made that choice, do I think that Adam would have lived or died? I don't think it means either. He could have lived or he could have died regardless of my choice, but I'm thankful that God brought me to that point where I could clearly see in my mind what He was asking me. I'm thankful I could clearly respond to Him because He is always with me. He is always there. He is always with every one of us and is always trying to draw us closer to Him.

I was confirmed as a deacon in January of 1999 and by the fall of 2000, I remember that God was continuing to work in my life and continuing to grow me through circumstances like I have just related, through continuing study in His Word and time in prayer.

We had started our small group again. We got back into full gear when the fall kicked off. I remember we were talking about prayer.

I would wake up and I would pray as I was getting ready for work each day, and I would have to get up pretty early—like at

4:20—and I challenged my small group to get up fifteen to twenty minutes earlier to focus that time solely upon prayer and meeting with the Lord. I said I also would do that. I would get up at four to be an encouragement to the rest of the group. I remember getting up at four and spending time with the Lord and not doing anything else but being with the Lord and praying. It was through that time that I really felt God burdening me with going into full-time ministry.

I remember coming home from work one day and Laura was sitting on the driveway. I said, "What if I told you I'm going to be a pastor? I'm going to go into full-time ministry."

I really do not recall what her exact response was, but as we started talking about it, I began looking into what I would need to do, such as further schooling. In my background, I had no formal Bible education. I hold a bachelor's degree in economics, so I began looking at seminaries and other options.

I believe one of the reasons, in God's mercy and grace, why He brought us here is that Pastor Morlan had realized, later in his life, that the Lord was calling him into the pastorate and my being able to see how God used him and what a pastor did and what schooling was needed; all of those things were very helpful to me during this time. It was also my being able to talk to him and seeing the different possibilities and options where I could do schooling and continue to work. I had wondered how could I go to school and do all these things, because I had a family.

I ended up doing seminary through Liberty University's distance education program. I viewed lectures on video tape and with Pastor as my proctor, wrote my papers and mailed them in. I could converse with my professors through email or on the telephone. I feel this was a great program for me and my family. I have been able to continue to be the father and the husband God wants me to be, do the work He wants me to do, and be able to provide for my family and still continue the ministry I was doing, however limited that might have been because I had a full-time job.

I was accepted ay Liberty in December of that year and I began classes in January. It took about three months to accomplish what I felt the Lord was calling me to do.

In 2004, after being ordained, Pastor Scott was called to serve at another church in Frankfort, Illinois, and has, since this interview, left GFC to preside at that church.

****

TESTIMONY V

Laura Kircher, Pastor Scott's wife, has shared her experience of her salvation and her walk with our Lord and how He has effected changes in her life.

Although my salvation experience may not seem like an exciting or monumental one, it is by far the most important thing that ever happened to me.

After being married for a couple of years, we found we were expecting our first child. We were so thrilled and in awe of the miracle of a child growing inside me. We both knew in our hearts that it was because of God. Although I knew of God and Jesus, I longed to know more about the God who was growing life inside of me and I wanted my child to know about God. Scott and I decided to go to church. We found a great church in our neighborhood that was a Bible teaching church and I began to learn so much about God. But, for the first time in my life, as I was reading and learning God's Word, I realized that even though I was a pretty good person (good values, good marriage ... all the things I thought God would see as good), that really I was a sinner. I was lost and separated from God. I was in desperate need of a Savior. It was a lesson in humility as I realized that God loved me so much that He had to give His Son's life for me. I finally realized that to know God, I had to give my life to Jesus and have a personal relationship with Him. So I accepted Jesus as my Savior in early 1993 and confessed Him publicly to my church soon after. I started searching for something for my child, and in the process I received a life-changing gift for myself.

Since then, I have grown closer to God and learned so much about how He would have me live. I have been able to teach my three children from birth about the God who created them and His Son, Jesus, who had to die for them. What a privilege!

When asked to share a time in my life when I was most certain God was walking with me, would be in the fall of 2002. My husband Scott and I were sitting and talking together on our driveway when he asked me how I felt about him going to seminary to become a pastor. Although this was the first time he had mentioned God tugging at his heart to serve Him in this capacity, in my heart I knew this was where God was leading Scott and our family.

It has been a long road since that day in the driveway, but I have been learning so much. I have learned that sometimes God may be speaking to Scott, yet seem to be quiet toward me. At these times, I have learned to be patient and to trust God in how He is leading Scott. I have learned that submission to my husband means encouraging and supporting him and following him where God leads him. It also means obedience to God and believing that God will provide for our family through Scott and the plan He has for him.

Now, two years later, Scott has resigned his secular job downtown, has been attending seminary, and has been working at our church as a non-salaried pastor. Because God had provided a severance package from his old job, we did not need a paycheck until the end of the year.

As the end of the year came nearer, instead of being overly anxious, I could feel God's peace that there would be financial provision for us when the time came. I had concern that it would be difficult to find a pastoral position because Scott wouldn't be quite finished seminary by the time we would need an income. I had to turn over to the Lord my tendency toward anxiety and remind myself who was in control. Thankfully, throughout the year, God has given me a peace I have never known. He has made me so aware of His presence in my life.

God made it perfectly clear He didn't want Scott to go back to the type of job and income he had had. God wanted Scott in ministry, serving Him full time. So, we trusted in God to provide a pastoral position somewhere for Scott when we would need an income.

Although God waited until the very last month to reveal the next part of His plan for us, He blessed us beyond measure by providing a pastoral position at our own church. The blessing of being able to stay with the church family we love and serve in ministry brings me to my knees in praise!

****

TESTIMONY VI

Mike Brooks is one of the members of GFC who is also one of the small group leaders in our Bible study groups. He leads the group that Cheryl and I attend. He has shared his salvation testimony and his faith that he does not walk alone because Jesus is always with him.

I was very fortunate in that I was born to a Christian family. Both my parents were Christians. Of course, this meant that I attended church all of my life.

When I was a little kid we were a part of a church that was just starting. It was a Southern Baptist church in Channahon where my mother still lives. It was a small church and of the children in the church, I was probably the youngest. I had an older sister and later I would have a younger sister, but for now I was just about the youngest of all the children there. I saw the other kids, my friends, and my sister walk the aisle and make professions of faith. I saw them baptized; this went on time after time. Remember, I was the youngest and it was not that anyone was pressuring me, but I felt some pressure, I think, and so after church on a Sunday night, I talked to my dad about it and he read the Scripture and I made what I believed at the time to be a profession of faith. I thought I had asked Jesus Christ into my heart but, as it turned out many years later, it wasn't real. There was no conversion. I guess it was just an emotional experience or something. I was baptized and I went many, many years believing I was saved. I wasn't an evil person, but really wasn't saved.

I was probably in my late teens when I started to feel what I later learned was conviction. I didn't understand what it was at that time, but I felt an emptiness, an uneasiness, and then my life started to go in some directions it shouldn't have gone. That went on for quite a while and it wasn't until 1984, when I was twenty-five years old, that things began just falling apart for me. I had lost considerable weight. I was down to about 170 pounds, which for me, is quite a lot. I wasn't trying to lose weight. I was having trouble sleeping and got to the point that I could hardly sleep at all.

I was put through a series of events. My grandmother, whom I loved very much, died; I felt like everything was just kind of caving in on me. My dog died shortly before I finally came down to earth and I realized that this time was really conviction. I had been questioning my salvation and even my going to church. It wasn't all the time, but it was off and on. It had all just started to overwhelm me. That was when I had started to lose all that weight and couldn't sleep.

It was on Valentine's Day, 1984, that finally I couldn't handle it any more. There was no doubt in my mind what the problem was. It was on a Sunday night after church. I had called my pastor and he had come over to my house and even then, I was still wrestling with Satan. Satan was fighting with me. He did not want to lose my soul. It was a wild night, but ultimately I did accept Jesus Christ as personal Savior. I had asked Him into my heart and after that I began to actually experience a true conversion. Not that I didn't continue to fail, and I still do, but there is no question in my mind that I had experienced a true conversion and that I truly was saved. I have put weight back on, and sleep much better now and I have taken steps to get my life back in order. I am still taking those steps.

I had been attending church all of my life, with only a few short periods when I wasn't, but I had never had any interest or desire to study God's Word. If I was in Sunday school class and someone would ask me to read Scripture, I would, but on my own I had no interest in it. Just having been around the preaching of the Word of God, I knew some facts and I knew some history of the Bible. I could find any book in the Bible, but it wasn't real to me. It was not until I was truly saved that the Word of God came to life. I have never gotten over that and now I consider myself a student of the

Word of God; if I had the time, I could study the Bible constantly because I never get tired of it.

That was the first thing I noticed, that the Word of God became a living organism, that it was fascinating, it was real to me, and it was life. Of course, I was still subject to Satan's attacks and I am still subject to failure, but I learned how to rebound, how to ask for forgiveness and ask for help in overcoming areas of weakness. Before this, I would just go merrily through life and let circumstances and the details of life dictate everything as opposed to having a true relationship with God.

I know the Lord is with me in all I do and I have a story I believe is fascinating, although it is somewhat of a sad story in certain parts.

I was saved in 1984 and Karen and I already knew each other at this point, although we were not married. We married shortly after that.

We had our older son, Tim, and then later on in 1992, Jordan, our younger son, was born. Shortly after he was born we discovered he had a problem with his eyes. He had a condition that is called aniridia. Not many people have heard of it. It is a very rare condition. He is legally blind, although he has some vision.

That was a challenge for us and he has many other difficulties related to that condition. It took a lot of effort and expense, but we were able to come into contact with people who were familiar with blindness and we networked with other organizations. We were eventually able to come to grips with all of that. We found creative ways to teach him, because it was a challenge to teach him due to his vision. Finally, we thought we had mastered this and were fairly well versed on meeting his needs. Then something happened on October 9, 1995.

I remember this vividly because it's his brother's birthday. Karen had been out in Baltimore. The ministry we were part of had a women's seminar and she attended that with some other ladies; our two sons were staying at my parent's house. I had picked her up at the airport and, after dropping Karen off, I was on my way to pick up the boys when she called me in the car and told me something was wrong with Jordan and that she didn't have any details. She didn't seem to be particularly alarmed. She is much more emotional than I, so she obviously didn't realize the severity of it either.

When I get to my parents' house, there is an ambulance in the driveway; I went in and saw Jordan. They had him lying on the couch and he had an unusual reddish color and a blank stare on his face. He was unresponsive and looked really bad. They didn't really know what had happened. He had been watching a movie and because of his vision he sits really close to the TV. He had fallen over backwards and that's all that my parents knew—that they thought he had hit his head. They were examining his head and weren't really finding anything wrong. They didn't see anything that was obviously wrong. My parents thought he may have just lost his balance and hurt his head, but we could see concern in the faces of the paramedics. They knew something more was wrong than what was apparent to the rest of us.

As I rode with Jordan in the ambulance to the hospital, he lost consciousness. When we got to the hospital, it was similar to a scene on TV—the staff were running frantically back and forth, grabbing things, and throwing stuff around. I had no idea what was going on, but I could see the seriousness on their faces. He was twitching and they explained to me that he was having a seizure. I had never witnessed one and could see the panic in their faces. He was losing his ability to breathe, so they put him on a respirator. This was just a little three-year-old boy and they put a big tube down his throat, so now he was on life support. I couldn't believe what I was seeing. It was so dire that when Karen finally got to the hospital, they had a woman who was like a chaplain waiting by Jordan's door to bring Karen in because it apparently looked pretty bad, at least to them.

They soon realized what was wrong was beyond their ability to diagnose or handle. He was at a hospital in Joliet and they made arrangements at Christ Hospital in Oak Lawn, which was better equipped for children. They sent him in another ambulance to Christ Hospital with a doctor, a respiratory therapist, and a nurse. Karen and I drove over there; by now it was very late at night or early in the morning. When we got there, it didn't seem that everyone was quite so panic-stricken, but there were several people always coming in and out of his isolation room in the pediatric intensive care unit. They still couldn't figure out what was wrong. He was continuing to have seizures and was able to breathe somewhat on his own, but they put him on the respirator because he could not breathe adequately on his own.

They were testing him for all kinds of things. They were questioning us because we had explained that we thought he might have hit his head. I guess they had to do that in case someone is beating up their kid. They tested him for rheumatic fever and chemicals, they questioned whether he might have gotten into some kind of chemicals or something like that. This went on and on.

It was sometime early in the morning, maybe six o'clock, that things finally began to calm down to the point that they explained what they were going to be testing for and that they really did not know what was causing the unusual seizures. With medication, they got the seizures to stop, but there were other things in the preliminary testing they had done and they still did not know what was wrong. At that point they were just going to wait until the next day's technicians arrived to perform the next tests. They didn't start until eight or nine in the morning, so we had a few hours to just sit and wait.

This was the most terrified that I have ever been in my life, without a doubt. Nothing can even come close. I felt I should be praying for him, but was just so gripped with fear and anguish I could hardly pray. In the room there was so much equipment that there was only one chair and they had to put some of the equipment on that. There was nowhere to sit, so we just sat on the floor and tried to pray. There came upon us a powerful experience of the presence of the Holy Spirit. We were sitting on the floor, scared to death, broken; it was as if God had come to us and put His arms around us. We felt like the Holy Spirit was saying, *"I know you can't pray right now. I am going to do it for you."*

It was still quite a while before Jordan started doing any better, but we were able to calm down and rationalize and get ourselves together, because there were some very important decisions to be made over the next few days. We had to gather ourselves together and I just don't know how a parent could do that if they were lost.

I was so riddled with pain and fear I couldn't even pray; the Holy Spirit made intercession on our behalf and prayed for us. We just know He did.

They continued to test him for all kinds of things, but could find nothing else. The respirator kept monitoring him and he continued to regain the ability to breathe on his own until finally they determined, after about thirty-six hours, he no longer needed it.

He still had many, many problems, and we still had a long way to go. He was in the hospital for a long time, maybe ten days, and since then, has been back in the hospital several more times.

One other thing I wanted to share was that after they had diagnosed him with having epilepsy, they found his was a very complicated case. They test with an electroencephalograph (EEG) which means they put electrodes on his head and try to have him sleep deprived so he can sleep during the test. This is how they can obtain the best readings.

Jordan's EEG is extreme. I guess they are very bizarre. As the doctors read them, they say his EEG looks like a person who has uncontrollable seizures. There are some people who have uncontrollable seizures. They medicate them as best they can, but they just cannot get them under control. We have seen five or six neurologists to date.

Then he had another seizure. It was probably about an hour long. He had to go to a hospital, and then they took him back to Christ Hospital. We battled with this for several years. Finally, one day, we heard through the Epilepsy Foundation about a doctor at Rush-Presbyterian St. Luke's hospital. They recommended him and although it took a while, we were able to get Jordan in to this doctor. After tests and evaluation, he felt Jordan's medication needed to be changed. Jordan had been on two different types of medication and the doctor decided we would take him off one and leave him on the other. He increased the dosage and since then Jordan has had just one more seizure. He has done blood work on Jordan and has modified the medication; it has been about three-and-a-half years and Jordan has not had an outward clinical seizure.

He has since been admitted into the hospital for testing using a video EEG. This is where they take him off his medication and glue the electrodes to his head because they must stay attached for an extended period of time. He lies in a bed while they have a camera observing him. They want to witness and record a seizure. He was in the hospital for a little longer than a week and it took several days before he had a seizure. I suppose the doctor learned things to help give Jordan the correct dosage and treatment. That was the last seizure we know of. A number of doctors have said his seizures would never be fully controlled, but we have never believed that.

There have been a great many people praying for Jordan. The ministry we were involved in before coming to Grace Fellowship has its parent church in Baltimore and they have several large prayer chains with thousands of people praying for him. People from my parent's church and countless others were praying. Although these doctors are highly trained and intelligent, and educated people have said the seizures would never be controlled, we know that God can say, *"I can control them."*

We have seen He has done exactly that.

Based on further testing, they say he has electro-graphic seizure activity in his brain, which explains some of his actions—but that kind of seizure does not damage the brain, as clinical seizures will.

We prayed to the Lord for the right doctor and the Lord led us to him. We prayed that He would get Jordan's seizures under control and He has done all that and more. We knew what all the doctors were seeing, but our faith was in God and He has never taken His eyes off Jordan.

I know God has a specific plan for Jordan's life and He stopped the seizures to put His plan in place.

****

TESTIMONY VII

Simon Luming's testimony of salvation is somewhat unique in that his coming to understand was different from the average person's experience. Simon also proved he always knew the Lord was with him throughout his life with his wonderful testimony about love.

I'm here to talk a little bit about my family and what God has done in our family.

I cannot recall exactly when I became a Christian, because I've been in a church all of my life. I say I became a Christian early in life. I never knew life without knowing God was there because my parents were Christians. It probably came to pass in high school where I really started to understand what the gospel was about. I never doubted the truth of it, but I think the true impact of forgiveness is that God loves us unconditionally, that we can't work our way to God. Growing up in a church, I thought I had to do stuff to be a good Christian and get to heaven. That's bad, because there is nothing you can do to satisfy God. We fail all the time and therefore, my self-worth was very low quite often in high school. With the way our Sunday school program was designed, they taught us how to say it and do it, and I knew all about it. But there was something different about how God was leading me closer to Him. He really started to mature me and I began to understand I needed to seek after Him.

This was in my teen years. I had to accept God's unconditional love. I think that's something I never did because I was trying to work to please Him; my self-worth was terrible because I thought I was a bad person every single time I sinned or did something wrong.

In post-college, I really started to feel the freedom God gives, not freedom to sin, but freedom from sin and the guilt that comes when you sin. I don't know how many people experience that, but I imagine people who grew up in a church experience it—the guilt or a sense of low self-worth because you had to find a way to please God. So I am thankful for the great impact of the gospel in terms of how it reaches to others. I have a perspective on that: it began when I got to Grace Fellowship Church and I think I really started to understand why God came for us because He loved us so deeply and I truly needed that. I didn't have to serve in the church to earn His salvation.

My family was very involved in church. My mom was the choir director, my dad was a deacon for a long time, and both my sisters were part of the beginning of the youth group. I was kind of dragged along, thinking this is what I'm supposed to do. Before I came to Grace Fellowship, I did a lot of my ministry leading Bible studies, leading worship out of duty, and didn't have the same kind of joy I have now. Now I don't feel I have to do it, I want to do it. I want to be close to God. I want others to see who He is, so consequently I experience much greater joy now that I understand what Jesus did for me and how it affects me in my life.

I know I never walk alone because it was God who led me to Caryn. I know He has always been there for me and now, He is here for both of us.

I met Caryn while at college. We were both part of the same Christian fellowship. I don't know how this is going to sound; sometimes I wonder how it all shook down. It must have been God. I have to admit I was pretty immature when I chose to date her. I think both of us were pretty immature. I'd been a Christian for a while, and she had just become a Christian so I don't know if the attraction is what led us to a lot of things, but I think God perfected our love for each other and no doubt God had a lot to do with putting us in each other's lives. People probably say we are pretty much a different type of couple. We had to have some of the opposite things too and I tend to be more emotional, and she a lot more practical and down to earth. So that is something we are working through. We compliment each other that way. I say we wouldn't be where we are if God did not continue to drive us to grow in Him. She has learned a lot from me and I've learned a ton from her. I have to say that God had a lot to do with what happened, even though the way it began was pretty immature, human-type stuff, like the physical attraction and feeling secure with each other.

Of course, when you're in college, it is a little bit different. There's less pressure because you can just kind of hang out. When you are out of college or in the work place, you have to go through all the pressure of asking someone for a date. But we lived in the same dorm and spent a great deal of time just sitting around and talking with each other.

I remember when I asked Caryn to marry me, although I don't remember the exact date. I remember I had already bought the ring. I hadn't actually planned a specific time to ask. I think I had targeted a time some three or four months down the road from when I actually asked her. I didn't even know I was going to ask her until about two hours before I did.

We had already gone out to eat and we were getting ready to go to an all-campus worship where all the Christian groups get together for worship time. I just decided, well, why wait? So I told her I had to go and pick up something from the house where I was staying. We drove by there and I ran in and grabbed the ring.

I'm not sure how it got started. I believe we just started joking around about marriage and I said, "Oh. We should just go over to the courthouse and get married now."

We just laughed it off and then we drove over for me to pick up the ring and she was wondering where we were going. We then drove to the courthouse and stood out front. It wasn't open, so we were just there at the corner of the courthouse and I asked her to marry me and she was extremely embarrassed, but very happy about it. Our getting together was based on our insecurities. It was after that when we started to learn we find our security in Christ.

I think we both had to grow through this. I don't think our getting together was due to Christian maturity; but fortunately, God taught us through that time and showed us a great deal of mercy because, as everyone knows, the first couple of years sometimes are difficult; living with a person and learning about all the different parts of them. But God showed us much grace and taught us how to manage. We really should not have to go to a lot of classes about marriage because it is all there in the Bible and we just have to follow it. Unfortunately, when we are emotional, it becomes difficult to follow it. We have to force ourselves to listen to the Holy Spirit telling us what to do. We need to listen and then follow through with our love for each other.

Caryn and I were married January 3, 1998.

I want to talk a little bit about Caryn and me, as we were getting ready to have children. We decided to go ahead and have children, although we thought originally that we were going to wait five years. The desire came a little bit earlier, so when we got pregnant, we were really excited and telling everybody. Then, when we found out just shortly into the pregnancy, approximately seven or eight weeks, that Caryn had miscarried, we were devastated. It was tough. I offer everyone this advice: wait before telling other people, because by the time people were congratulating us, we were telling them we had miscarried. It was awkward for everybody. It was really tough and so we prayed a lot. Caryn had to go through a whole procedure to get that miscarriage taken care of and she went through extreme pain when the thing actually occurred. God got her through it and taught us a lot about helping each other and me assisting her, not understanding her pain sometimes. She had a pain I have never seen anybody experience. I was fumbling because I wasn't able to do anything about it. God helped me take care of it. He tried to teach us a lesson. After that, we tried to get pregnant again and once again it was a tough trial—over a year and a half of trying and not able to conceive. Then Caryn talked to her doctor and her progesterone was tested. The level was way below what it could possibly be to conceive.

Caryn was just about to start on some hormones. We were really concerned about not being able to conceive because we didn't want to go through too many alternative means to get pregnant. We were scared about the whole thing, so we prayed that God would work things out. Just before she started on the progesterone, sure enough, she became pregnant—which was almost impossible. We only tried once in the weeks prior to that and didn't expect anything; plus, we were told we couldn't get pregnant with the level she was at. But she did conceive and we have Emily, who is now a year and a half old. We treasure her very much, knowing that God was teaching us a lesson about His care for us and about His patience. To finish the story, as we were planning to have another child, we prayed before we started that God would help make it easier; that God would make it a little simpler instead of our having to wait that long and go through those trials. Sure enough, after the first couple of times we tried, Caryn became pregnant with our second child. So we don't know yet if he is a she, or she is a he, but we're extremely thankful that God taught us to do that even though it was a difficult time. We definitely have a greater awe of God's care for us because of our situation surrounding the pregnancy with Emily and her birth and our conception of our second child. We definitely give God all the credit; we're glad we were able to follow Him and He was able to pull us through even though we had no clue what we were doing.

****

TESTIMONY VIII

Adam McCune is the current youth director of Grace Fellowship Church. He was born on August 27, 1980 and grew up in the Chicagoland area. He became a believer July 11, 1991, was baptized January 5, 1992, and first visited Grace Fellowship on Easter Sunday of 1994. Adam was actively involved in the church's youth group, the Image, and the high school drum line. Upon graduating high school he attended Cedarville University where he earned a degree in Bible and graduated with honors. He spent the summer of 2002 in South Africa at an orphanage and returned in July of the same year to become the church's youth director. Adam is a history buff who loves to read, play football, and teach drum lessons to high school and junior high students.

I should start by saying I grew up in a Christian home. Both my mother and father were faithful believers. Both sets of my grandparents were also believers, so my earliest memories are of being in church and being involved with the kids program, being parts of plays, and asking questions ("Mom, why do we do this? Why do we do that?"), and receiving truthful answers.

Even though I had grown up in that environment, I believed that to be active in church was what it took to be pleasing to God. For years, even as a child, that was my understanding of what it meant to be somebody who would go to heaven. Even as a seven and eight year old, I thought that if I died I would go to heaven because my parents went to church and my grandparents went to church and so did I. I was in Sunday school and I knew all the songs. That was my understanding and the one person in my life who God used to really share the truth with me, even though I had been hearing the gospel in its truth the whole time, was my grandmother, Wilma. Wilma was my mom's mom. Grandma Wilma moved to Tennessee when my grandpa retired, so I only got to see her once in the month of July. I would stay in Tennessee with them. Every night my grandma would read her Bible and you could tell in everything she did that she just loved the Lord. She was the kind of person who, if you had a question, it didn't matter what time of day it was or how deep the question, you always got an honest answer. I was always asking her difficult questions like, "Who is going to hell?", because I would hear about what hell was and what heaven was. "Who is going to heaven? Who is going to be with Jesus when He comes back and brings His people home to heaven?"

She would explain to me that it would be those who had accepted Jesus, who said, "Jesus, I need Your forgiveness, for what You've done for me. I need that forgiveness for my sin and I believe that You are the Son of God and that You died for my sins and You are alive again. You arose from the dead."

I had to ask myself the difficult question: "I haven't done that necessarily. So what does that mean to me?"

She had enough love from God to say the truth.

"Son, if you have not done that, you are not protected eternally. You are not in God's family."

But she would also tell me that God wants me to believe in Him. When I was eleven, I remember talking to her at the kitchen table. She was doing dishes after lunch and I had asked those questions again and she repeated herself and I knew that I was supposed to just give up and just let God forgive me of my sins and confess them to Him and I needed to let Jesus save me—not myself, not my church—but let Jesus do it. I had struggled with that and for that whole week, every night, it was harder and harder to sleep. Even as a ten year old, it was very hard to sleep because I knew if I died tonight, if I didn't wake up, I would not be in heaven. I would be in hell.

Right after that happened, I went into a guest bedroom and my brother and I got into a fight as was typical. We fought a lot back then. After that happened, I felt terrible. I realized I had just sinned. I think it was the first time that I really realized that I had just done something wrong. I went back into my room, shut the door, got down on my knees, and knew I had to confess my sins.

"Jesus, I sinned before You today and I've done it a lot before. I realize that I need You to forgive me of my sin. I ask that You take over my life because You are Lord. You are God. I'm asking You to forgive me, not just now, but forever as only You can do."

That afternoon, July 11, 1991, I accepted Christ as my Lord and Savior and knew immediately when I said amen, it was like I was a different person. I couldn't say it was an emotion; it wasn't like chills going down my spine. But I could sense a weight was gone, like I had been freed from something. Later on in life, I would understand that at a much deeper level, but certainly as a kid I knew that something was different and I knew God did forgive me because this was the first time and probably one of the only times in my life that when I walked into my brother's room, he apologized. He was a believer before I was. Even though he was younger, he accepted Christ earlier. He apologized and I thought, "This is crazy."

We were actually apologizing to each other so God had to be doing something miraculous because that had never happened before. From that day forward, my life changed eternally. I could say that I died that day, and now I belong to Christ. I am His because He saved me that day.

I went back into the kitchen. My grandma wasn't done with the dishes and I said to her, "You're wrong. I'm going to heaven now."

I explained to her what I had just done. A few months later, both my brother and I were baptized and began our walk of obedience.

Our relationship didn't change for a little while. We were still at each other as brothers are when you live together. We annoyed each other, but we had many moments after that day. We understood that God was doing something. We both decided on the same day that we wanted to go forward and be baptized and we asked the pastor if we could do that.

We didn't have deep spiritual conversations, but we could pray together.

My brother had a time when he rebelled against the Lord. It hurt me very much. But in the years since then, when he joined the Marines, God used the drill sergeants to teach him priorities in life because he realized that he needs God and even though once you are saved you are always saved; certainly, he was not following obediently. He has since turned his life around and then he got out of the Marines (July 2004). He is going to attend Bible school and prepare himself for the ministry. We now get along better than most brothers I know. There was a rocky time, but I think God used it to bring us closer together.

There was a time in my life when, though it seemed like I might have been alone, because of God, I did not walk alone.

I was one day shy of going off to college. College for me was an incredibly large struggle during my senior year of high school. The idea of leaving home and my comfort zone scared me. I had always lived in this area, so I had no friends in any other part of the world or even the state and here I was thinking of going to school out of state. I was about to go someplace totally foreign to me. I was going to a college that, even though it was a godly college, there was nobody I knew who had ever gone there before. It wasn't just as if I was the only one in my family going; it wasn't like I was moving to a new area—there was nobody I knew there. There were no friends from my high school going; no one from my church who had gone before and was going back. This was going to be a time for me to blaze a trail. I knew God wanted me at that college. I knew He would teach me what I needed to learn in preparation for ministry. Even though I knew that, I was still scared to death.

I remember what I said to God that day my dad and I pulled out of the driveway to go to school. "God, You better know what You're doing because I'm leaving everything back there in that driveway. I'm leaving my friends, my church, and my family. I am leaving everything I know. I'm leaving the roots I've dug in my life. I'm leaving them for something I haven't got a clue will work or not."

I was extremely scared and I struggled and I admit that struggle lasted for quite a while. Yet, I knew that when I arrived at that college I was going to be determined to make good friends and be as friendly as possible so I could meet new people and give it a chance.

I knew I would miss home and that it would not be the same for a while. I knew I would trust God was going to put me in the right positions to meet the right people. In my freshman year I met some of those who I believe will be my lifelong friends and I met them during the first few days.

I remember this as being a strange experience. I literally walked into a guy who I had been eyeing during the first week of school and who I thought looked like he was a nice kid. He looked like somebody I could get along with. I went and I shook his hand and I dragged him into my room. I said, "I need a friend. You want to be my friend?"

That's how our friendship started. His name was Mike Akers. As time went on I made other friends that I thought God was really going to use in my life. Even then I still felt I didn't know what God was doing. Even though I understood my classes and was getting good grades and I had people around me whom I was really getting along well with, I found myself trying to figure out what God was doing. I found myself asking, "God, what are You doing? Is my role just to go to class for four years?"

I spent my entire first year looking for a church. I should include in this testimony that I joined a drum line in high school and have always played drums. I love to play drums and I had to quit that in my senior year to be well prepared for college. I was upset about that because I love music so much. Little did I know that God would give me a break and use drums to provide for me.

Basically, my entire college experience was an experience that formed my life and ministry to this day. I was looking for a church. I visited different churches several times in a row to get a feel for their family. I talked to the pastors and asked, "How does the church operate?"

I was looking for that place where I could not just enjoy it, but I could give back to it; I could invest in it. I believed that if I was to grow there, that I needed to be almost a visiting member of that church even though I already had a church back home.

I had a friend who said to me, "Hey! I heard you play drums. My dad is the worship leader at a church and he's looking for a drummer. Would you be willing to try it out?"

I said, "Drums can be a little touchy in churches, but if he is be comfortable with me, I'm comfortable with it."

I went to this little church called Hillside Chapel in Beaver Creek, Ohio. Little did I know that God was going to bring me to my church family there—and it was through drums. I played the drums there. As soon as I played the first week, the pastor not only said, "We would like you to come to this place for your college time." I sensed from the Lord this was a place I wanted to be in. Then the pastor added, "And we'll help you financially."

They paid me enough money to support myself through college—God provided a church family and an income all in one shot—that just was really cool. When I got home that summer I said, "You know what? I'm going to take a risk."

I still had not told my dad this so I guessed he would eventually find out that I spent my entire summer savings on a drum set instead of tuition. I, like the foolish young guy I was, thought I would make my living on drums or something. I said, "I'm going to buy a drum set with all the money I saved from my entire summer's work."

I bought a nice set of drums, one of the best you could get. I went back to school with it and finally told my dad that I had a set of drums even though he didn't know the price. When I got there I thought, *"Now what did I do? I have no place to put it. I am only going to play at one church, which even though they are providing for me, it's not going to equal what I paid for it."*

I remember getting a phone call one day from a student worship leader for the praise band that plays in chapel on Fridays. The students run the entire chapel time on Fridays.

He said, "I've got a guy who plays drums, but he's a multimedia major and he has decided that for his internship he wants to help run the sound system. He doesn't want to play drums, so I need a drummer. I asked around and your name came up. What do you think?"

I was thinking, *"I know this band. They're really good and they play in front of three thousand students once a week. I don't know if I'm ready for that. But I'm not going to say no."*

So I said, "Hey, is the pope Catholic? Of course he is. Hey, I'm playing. I'm not going to turn this down."

I met John. That year formed the entire pace for my college experience. I was able to learn what worship was through John—not just play drums but also learn about worship. I made friends with some of the chaplains and some of the really godly men on campus who were older than me. Now I had mentors, something that few other students had. Here I was, somebody who left everything I knew to go to a place where I knew nothing and no one and God had me surrounded with the leading men on campus. Not only that, but they are mentored by one of the vice presidents and by many of the faculty. I was meeting some of the godly men and women who have served and have been successful not only in ministry but in what they do. They shared so much wisdom with me. Somehow, through that exposure, people got to know me. They have a ministry there where seven men—seven students—lead a Wednesday night chapel service and a Sunday night chapel service for students who don't have cars and can't get off campus. These seven men are responsible for teaching. They preach on those nights and put together the entire service, but they are elected by the student body. The students nominated me for that and I was asked to share my testimony so they could affirm and then vote on me for the group. Of course, I was just going crazy. I didn't know what I was up for but, like everything else, I just dove in. I knew God had made this opportunity, because I had done nothing to get it. It wasn't on my mind, so I was just going to go and share myself and if the Lord wanted me to be in the ministry, He would impress it on the hearts of the students. Sure enough, I shared my testimony and they elected me to be one of the seven students.

Now I was with six great guys who had a lot of leadership potential and it is great to hear from them even now. Three are studying to be pastors, one is a senior pastor, another is a youth pastor. I see where they are going and how God is using them and it all started right then.

The vice president of Christian ministries is like the campus pastor or the campus chaplain. He has thirty years of pastoral experience and he was sharing that with us. Intensely, for a year, he mentored us. Because of drums, I was now playing in a worship band on Fridays. I was able to minister to students. I wouldn't say it was so much a popular role; as much as it was an impact type of role. I wasn't popular on campus, but I was able to make a spiritual impact. Students would come to me with their concerns and I could pray with them and follow up with them. I was able to set a spiritual pace with these other guys. We helped raise thirty-plus thousand dollars for an orphanage in Africa which, little did I know, God would open that experience for me to visit that place and talk to those people and say, "Yeah, I was there when we raised this for you."

They still are just blown away that college students would raise thirty grand.

When I graduated, I cried all the way home because I felt the same way I did when I left for college. I said, "God, You better know what You're doing because I'm leaving everything here and all of my friends. Even though I know I'm going home, I'm also leaving home."

That's when I think it all hit me. In those four years, not only did I not walk alone, but God had completely paved a path I didn't plan on. I literally didn't do anything to make it happen. It was almost as if there was a wave and I was on a surfboard and somehow I caught it and rode it and God used me to make an impact. What is even cooler now is I have gone back a couple of times and I talk to students and they say, "Are you Adam? Are you Adam McCune? I remember when you said this or that" and they ask me about my life and how I'm doing and I am able to minister to students even now. I may only go there once in maybe three or four months.

What I learned there was that it was so insane to do it, to leave everything I knew. But I had to trust God so much there was no way He would not bless it. God knew what He was doing and I say to this day that going to that college and just trusting God, even though it was more like kicking, screaming, and being dragged there, I would still say that was the best decision I ever made. Those four years have given me a passion to know that from now on if I have to do that again in some way, I am doing it because I know He is going to open a door beyond what I don't know is waiting, but I know I will not walk alone even then.

****

TESTIMONY IX

My wife, Cheryl, has a story we both could tell, but she is better at remembering some of the important details I would have overlooked. It is our story and the Lord's hand in our lives is, I believe, quite evident along with His great love, grace, and mercy. Her salvation story lays some important groundwork for explaining our need to pray almost constantly for our son, Mike. It is also about our only son, Mike, and how God's mercy was manifest in the answer to our fervent prayers for him.

My dad died when I was six and right after he passed away, my uncle Ed, my mom's brother, decided it was a good time for us to start going to church. He looked around for us and found the Berwyn United Lutheran, just two blocks from our house. We used to walk there every Sunday. So I was raised a Lutheran. At six years of age I didn't really know what was going on. At that time church was just a drag for me, something to do on Sunday mornings and I couldn't wait to get home because it just didn't mean too much to me. I was baptized when I was nine at Berwyn United Lutheran because I had never been baptized when I was a baby, which is what their beliefs are. After I got to be a teenager, we began to kind of just sluff off church, so I never really got back into it until after I got married.

We began to be friends with Sue and Len Ackerley. I had met Sue when I worked at Field Enterprises in downtown Chicago in 1967 and part of 1968. She and I had gotten to be good buddies and sometime after I returned to Illinois with Vic after he was discharged from the Army, they invited us to their house in Streamwood one night. Then we had them out our house and we kept in touch that way. They invited us to church with them for a Sunday service a number of times. We accepted their invitation and began going all the way up to Streamwood on Sunday mornings to attend church with Sue and Len. It was the Grace Bible Church with Pastor Barker. He was a super, super nice guy; a good preacher.

He preached about salvation and I thought, *"Well, I'm already saved. I've been baptized."*

But he was preaching something that was altogether different and much easier than what I thought it was going to be.

One night when we came out to their house, Pastor Barker was there and he asked me and Vic, "Do you know where you're going when you die?"

I said, "Well yeah. I'm probably going to go to heaven. I've been a good person and I've not done too much wrong."

He answered, "No. That's not it at all."

He told us about salvation and that all you have to do is accept Jesus Christ as your Savior and that is the end of it. I thought, *"No, this is just too easy. There has to be a catch to it."*

I did accept Jesus then, but was really skeptical because I thought there must be more to it—that was what I was taught as a Lutheran. You have to do works and get baptized and go through confirmation classes and take communion. I don't know if Vic accepted the Lord then or not. Maybe he just went through the motions. This was probably in the late seventies. Mike was just a kid. I think he was eight or nine.

Then some years later, I think in about 1985, Scott Willis, who was the pastor of Parkview Baptist Church, was encouraging Vic to go to church because Vic got saved by Pastor Willis. So we started going there. We learned quite a bit from Pastor Willis. I guess I had to sort of get re-saved because I was not living the life of a Christian. Vic and I were still bar hopping and taking our poor kid with us to bars and drinking and being just regular party animals. This definitely was not a Christian life, but then after Vic got saved, I kind of came around.

Pastor Willis was called to another church and we stuck around at Parkview Baptist in Mokena and that's when Pastor Michael Richmond came in and when I really saw the light. There were a lot of really nice people there and when he first started, Mike Richmond was a really good preacher. But later it got really crumby over there and there were problems with Richmond.

But Mike Richmond had baptized us both soon after he got there and there was a change in both our lives. There was a definite change in my life. I did not ask for it. It wasn't my decision. I didn't say, "I'm going to change now that I'm a Christian." It just came over me and there I was, I was changed. That was the Holy Spirit working in my life.

Our church split up. Parkview Baptist church split up. There were a lot of nasty attitudes and a lot of different stuff going on. Our church was all but ready to close the doors. There were only a few dozen people left.

Then Bill Hosh found a church that was just starting up; I guess in someone's home in New Lenox. It was Pastor Robert Morlan who was starting this fledgling church and Bill told Pastor Morlan that our church was breaking up and maybe we could work out a deal where he could merge both our church and his church. That is what we did and I've kind of grown in the Lord only because of Pastor Morlan, because I've really learned a lot from him and how to trust in the Lord a lot better.

My son, Mike, had gone to Turkey Run in Indiana one weekend to go canoeing on the river there and had fallen into the river which did him no apparent harm. However, a few weeks after his return, he noticed a very small mole-like growth just under his left nostril. It felt like a big pimple, but after a year, when it still had not gone away, he went to the doctor. The doctor tried to cut it out and that's when it became very aggravated and started spreading like wildfire across my son's upper lip, up his nostril, and along the side of his nose. He looked like he had a piece of cauliflower growing out of the side of his nose. We took him to doctor after doctor; they tried to burn the stuff off with lasers and he would be in such great pain. His face was all bloody after each surgery and before the burns could completely heal, this stuff would return and grow with even greater vengeance, increasing faster in size and area. They had no idea what this stuff was and would try again with the laser surgery only to see the growth increase even faster. It was taking over my son's face and was beginning to grow up his nose and into his mouth and throat. We were praying and praying for a solution. We had our entire church praying for him. We put him on everyone's prayer list we talked to about him.

One day when he was in the hospital for another surgery, I met a lady in the waiting room. She had a uniform on, so I asked if she was in the Army. She said she was in the Salvation Army. I told her about my son and she told me she was going to a prayer service that evening and would have the folks pray for Mike. There was going to be about three hundred people there.

When the doctor came to talk, we went to a private area and that's when he told us this was the last time he could work on Mike because the treatment wasn't working. He said if we couldn't get help for Mike, he might have as much as six months to live because this was heading up his nose, into his sinuses, over the roof of his mouth, between his teeth, and down his throat. His face was hideously covered with it. Because of all the laser surgeries, they had welded his mouth almost closed. He only had a gap of about an inch or less left and had to shove food in with one finger and could only drink through a straw. Every time he coughed we prayed he wasn't choking because we knew of no way to help him if that happened.

Only days later we got a call from the doctor. He was a wonderful Jewish doctor at the Illinois Masonic hospital on the north side of Chicago. He was really excellent. He really cared about Mike and wasn't going to give up on him. He sent us to a new doctor, Dr. Joan Gudardt. Joan, I guess, is a foreign form of the name John, because when they told us it was Dr. Joan Gudardt, we were expecting a woman and here comes this guy with this name tag saying Joan.

He was very excited when he entered the examination room.

He said, "I've had one patient like you when I was an intern thirty some years ago."

He said he knew what Mike had and told us he could cure him. I just broke down in tears.

He took a biopsy from Mike's nose. He went to the lab and looked it over and came back and said, "Yes, I know what you have and I can cure you."

This was only about a week after I met the woman from the Salvation Army and she had asked these three hundred people to pray for us; we already had countless others telling others about our son and I don't know how many churches full of people were praying for my son.

They gave him a very expensive medication called Sporanex. It was like eight hundred dollars for a vial of pills, but I didn't care. Mike didn't have the money and no insurance so Vic and I sprung for it. You can't put a price tag on anything that important. Money was definitely not an issue.

He immediately started taking the pills and the growth just seemed to begin to dissolve; it was just disappearing and melting away. It took a couple of months, but after a while all that was left were the severe scars from all those laser surgeries. I just can't praise God enough. How wonderful it was for us to be lead to Dr. Gudardt. For him to have healed someone who had the same thing that Mike had was another blessing. Its name is blastomycosis. He was the only doctor who knew what Mike had.

Afterward, as Mike came to him for more checkups, doctors would come in from all over the country and from all over the world to see my son and ask questions. There were doctors who used interpreters because they did not speak English. They took pictures of my Mike and Dr. Joan told us that he was going to be in medical books so others around the world could be cured without going through what my son went through. I guess my son made medical history.

I have to say those were the worst two years my husband and I ever had, and certainly it was the worst time in Michael's life.

After all of this had gone away and was over, which was about six months, we took Mike to a plastic surgeon so work could be done on his mouth. They had to cut his mouth open and then sew it back up so it was wider like it was before. They did this twice. He had one side done and when that was healed fairly well, they did the other side. They wanted to wait for him to completely heal before discussing reconstructive surgery for his face.

God has really worked in his life and ours since this happened and now we are so much closer with each other. Our Lord not only worked in our lives, but on Mike's face. We were told his hideous scars could only be reduced and maybe eliminated by plastic surgery, but we and all our church friends and family continued to pray. After a few more years, Mike's face has healed so much that only minimal scarring remains and although plastic surgery will still be needed, it will not be major surgery, as we had feared. We hope and pray we can afford to help him receive the needed surgery soon, as he is still very self-conscious about it.

We had been praying for our son long before any of this happened, that God would intervene in Mike's life because he was a real party animal and was living a life that could have easily caused his untimely death. When blastomycosis hit him and he began to know in his heart that his chances of survival were not good, he returned to the Lord and prayed with us. I am sure he said prayers alone. Even now, when we travel somewhere with him, he asks his dad to pray for our trip before we leave. God did not cause this to happen to my son, but He used it as the two by four we prayed for to hit Mike in the head. He really got Mike's attention. I praise and thank God that He heard our prayers and saved our son, both spiritually and physically.

✼✼✼

TESTIMONY X

I could not write this without giving my testimony. God is the author who is using me to proclaim His hand in all His children's lives and we who are born again are all His children.

My salvation story is at least slightly unique, but nevertheless it was and always will be the greatest defining moment of my life. I praise the Lord for His promise to me of eternal life with Him in heaven and for His promise that He will never forsake me. I can tell a book's worth by myself of stories showing how many times I have known that He was not only walking with me, but those times when all hope seemed lost, except for the hope I had in Him, when He did much more than walk with me. My Lord carried me.

I was raised in the Catholic religion and because of their doctrinal teachings I grew up a very confused person and spent my time growing up as a very frightened child.

The most vivid memories that caused my fear were the prayers I had to memorize—for what circumstances and occasions I cannot even begin to remember—except for the Act of Contrition.

I was taught by the nuns in catechism class that Jesus died for my sin so I could be saved. The catch, as I perceived it, was that at the time of my death, a priest had to be present to administer the Last Rites. If this was not possible, then it was my responsibility to say the Act of Contrition just before my death so I would find the forgiveness I needed to get to heaven. If neither of these rituals were done, then God would judge me for my sins. Further confusing my young mind was being told that God could sentence me to hell or to purgatory, depending on whether I was being judged for only venial sins, which are minor ones, or for mortal sins which buy a one-way ticket to hell. As a child growing up a Catholic, I lived in constant fear I would not be able to recite the Act of Contrition, especially if I died in my sleep, and that I would suffer eternally in hell. I said that prayer every night for years before falling to sleep and many times spontaneously during the day, just in case I needed it.

In 1968 I returned home from Vietnam after being wounded in combat on the first of February. It was during my first convalescent leave from the military hospital at Fort Riley, Kansas that I met the woman I would fall in love with and marry later that same year.

Cheryl was one of a few young women who wrote letters to local boys serving in the military overseas and I was one of the guys with whom she chose to correspond. Her letters were all about stuff of interest to a local guy on what was happening back home. She wrote such that I thought I was the only guy she was writing to; only about a dozen or more other guys had the same impression. I wanted to meet this girl who did not get mushy with a guy she never met, yet made me feel as if she really cared enough to lift my spirits with her letters, so on February 17 I visited her for the first time at her home in Berwyn.

I asked her to marry me two short weeks later. She accepted and we wed on September 25, 1968. She returned with me to Fort Bliss, Texas and we lived in a mobile home off base until my discharge from active duty on May 29, 1969 when we returned to Berwyn.

We moved a few times since then and eventually purchased a home in Mokena where we still live today. It was in Mokena where I was saved.

I was a mentally troubled veteran who really needed intervention in my life and I knew not where to turn since I had, years ago, turned from the Catholic faith. Intervention came one evening in the 1980's.

I had gotten drunk and for reasons I cannot explain to this day decided to go on a headhunt. A headhunt in Vietnam was an unsanctioned patrol, which serves no government purpose. It is an excursion into the brush to seek out and kill enemy soldiers for one reason. The reason is to kill.

I had placed my guns in my van and headed down the streets of Mokena to kill I do not know who. Strangely, and most fortunately, there was not a living soul on the street and since it was a rather cold evening and I had the window open for a long period, I began to sober up. The realization of the great sin I was about to commit came to me in enough time for me to drive home and stow my guns. I then staggered over to the police station to turn myself in. I told the police officer about what I had done and to my surprise he did not arrest me. Officer McFadden was a Christian from Parkview Baptist Church in Mokena. He told me they could not arrest me for what I was going to do. I had to actually do something. He did tell me that it appeared to him I needed some help. He asked if I wanted to see a clergyman. I said yes and within the hour Pastor Scott Willis showed up and we sat together in a room while he ministered to me. The Lord was with me and was walking with me even before I knew Him. I was crying out for help and my Lord sent Pastor Scott Willis.

I am truly sorry I was so drunk I can not recall most of what was said except for the gist of the meeting. I remember that Pastor Scott led me through to my salvation. It was there in the Mokena police station that I confessed to the Lord that I was a sinner lost in my sin. I admitted I needed Him and accepted Jesus Christ, the Son of God and the Savior of man, as personal Lord and Savior. Thus began the first day of the rest of my life.

Some people experience great changes overnight. Others, due to stupidity and pigheadedness, require a great deal more time. I required a great deal more time. I was changed gradually over the next decade, but the Lord kept working in my life and as I gradually turned my life over to Him, He effected greater changes in me and He is not finished with me yet even today.

I have two stories to relate; the second having occurred in June 2005.

The first story happened to me a short time after my salvation experience and it dramatically affected my outlook.

It was about a year after I was saved that I believe the Lord was really watching over me. I credit God for saving my life.

We Never Walk Alone

I was working for Illinois Bell Telephone Company and on this day I was working on aerial telephone lines using a bucket truck. This is a vehicle with an extending arm which has a self-leveling unit on the end capable of holding a person and his tools. Fully extended, it can attain a height of thirty feet or more. Normally, when working on the edge of a busy street, it was common practice to park facing oncoming traffic so as to afford a degree of protection from other vehicles. I was forced to park with the traffic, due to the proximity of an intersection. The other way would have blocked the flow of traffic and caused a safety hazard for the other vehicles going in the opposite direction.

Hand soap and paper towels were kept in an outside compartment directly behind the driver's door. When facing traffic, this was the safest place to clean my hands without the worry of being sideswiped by a vehicle, since the truck was almost always at least a few inches or more on the street and not totally off the road. Since I had to face traffic this day, this compartment was on the traffic side of the vehicle.

I had just finished my work at about two-thirty and had dismounted from the bucket. I stowed and locked everything down and had only to retrieve the traffic cones from alongside the truck.

I began to step toward the compartment holding the hand cleaner, when I can only explain this as that I heard a voice inside my head say, "Go to the other side of the truck."

It was not an audible voice, like someone talking to another person, but more of a voice speaking to my soul. I do not know why, but I immediately began walking away from the street side of the truck toward the ditch. I did not consciously obey the voice. It was more as if I was compelled to obey the voice. No sooner had I taken a couple of steps when a northbound pickup truck lost his entire right front wheel assembly a few feet from me. The right front end of his truck hit the ground as the wheel assembly bounced off the driver's side of my truck only a split second before the passenger side of the pickup truck slammed into the driver's side of my truck, smashing it in something awful. All of this occurred only moments after I should have been standing in the midst of it. The jolt of the sudden sideways rocking of my truck made me almost jump out of my skin. The moment I looked at the damage I knew that it was only by the grace of God and that voice, which I believe He had something to do with, that I was still not only alive, but totally safe from harm.

The Lord said He would be with me and would always walk with me even when I fall down and fail in my effort to walk with Him. On that day, in that moment, He didn't walk with me. I believe He carried me to safety. I thank Him for that and praise Him for loving me so much that I can have hope for eternity in heaven with Him and His assurance that no matter what happens on earth, I will never walk alone. My Lord, Jesus, will always be with me.

I have one more story to relate, as this occurred while I am still in the process of collecting testimonies and completing this project.

On June 26, 2005, I experienced something that, when the entire story is told, can only be summed up as miraculous.

Actually, my experience began on the afternoon of Friday, June 24. I had been having indigestion, beginning the morning of that day, and it increased considerably by Friday evening. I spent that night trying in vain to alleviate what I thought was severe indigestion. I did not realize it at that time, but I was experiencing a heart attack. This continued to plague me with only temporary abatement until Sunday morning, June 26, 2005.

To set the stage for this, I digress to explaining the situation at our house.

We do not have central air conditioning, as our old house is hot water heated with radiators and since the outdoor temperatures were in the upper 90's with high humidity, Cheryl and I had been camping out in our living room where our two window air conditioners had been keeping the first floor at least tolerable. We only ventured upstairs to shower and dress and then hurried downstairs to the relative coolness of the first floor.

I was feeling considerably better by the time we awoke on Sunday morning, so we had a full breakfast of fried eggs, sausage links, white toast with real butter, and some strong regular coffee. We had all the foods that were not healthy to consume, so by the time I was getting dressed upstairs about thirty minutes later, my indigestion had returned with a vengeance.

I got myself downstairs only to find that Cheryl was in the bathroom—the room where the antacids were. I was hurting so bad by now I felt I could not wait for her to open the door and I decided to try a home remedy that my son had told me about. I remembered that he had said a capful of vinegar was supposed to alleviate heartburn almost immediately, so I went directly to the food cabinet to find some vinegar.

I was not wearing my glasses, which I need for nearsightedness and remembered that the vinegar was in a white plastic bottle, so I began tearing through the shelves searching for a white plastic bottle. I found one on the bottom shelf shoved all the way to the back. I was in such pain by now that I very quickly opened the cap, filled it with some of the liquid, and gulped it down. I remember that as I neared my mouth with this capful of what I thought was vinegar that I thought to myself, "Vinegar sure smells really bad."

By the time my mind registered the smell and associated it with ammonia, I was already swallowing the stuff. I felt it burning all the way down my throat as I got up from my kneeling position on the floor and sprinted to the kitchen sink where I managed to call out my wife's name and say something about badly needing help.

Cheryl was dialing 911 in a matter of seconds while I was head down in the kitchen sink trying desperately to make myself throw up the ammonia.

Cheryl told me sometime later that when the 911 operator heard what Cheryl told her I drank her reply was, "He drank WHAT?"

The operator had poison control on the line almost immediately and they instructed Cheryl to not let me vomit and get me to drink some milk immediately. My wife was at my side with a glass filled with milk and told me to stop sticking my finger in my throat and drink the milk, which I drank very fast. The effect was an immediate relief of some of the burning feeling, so I drank another glassful as my wife returned to the phone. An ambulance came in moments and the EMTs saw that this was more than poison ingestion. I was given two nitro tablets under my tongue by one of the ambulance people and was transported to Silver Cross Hospital in Joliet because poison control was located there.

I was administered an EKG at the emergency room and a doctor told me I was having a heart attack and was going to be transferred to Saint Joseph's Hospital on the west side of Joliet because they were better equipped to handle this. His associate, Dr. Ramadurai, was going to perform the procedure.

They had an operating room waiting for me and I was given an angiogram which determined that an artery which directly feeds the heart muscle was 100 percent clogged, so the doctor performed an angioplasty which opened my artery and a stent was permanently implanted at the clog. This opened the artery. I was taken to the cardiac ICU. The doctor told me the operation went well, but since I had been experiencing this heart attack since Friday, I could expect my heart to have suffered forty to seventy percent damage. This, I perceived, was not a good thing. In fact, I guessed that I might be permanently physically disabled from the damage.

I had asked Cheryl to call our pastor and tell everyone we needed their prayers. This she did even before I was operated on.

I was in the cardiac intensive care area from Sunday afternoon until I was released to go home on Wednesday, June 29.

On Tuesday evening, the night before I was hopeful of being released to go home, my heart was given an ultrasound test to determine the extent of the damage my heart had suffered. The doctor came into my room later that evening with the results in hand. He informed me that he was quite surprised. My heart had suffered almost no damage and he expected a full recovery in three to five months. He also told me there was no apparent damage to my esophagus from the ammonia ingestion.

I am now at home, comfortably recuperating, and working on this book.

This is my personal testimony—that God is always with me and the power in prayer is evident all over this story. It is God's mercy and love that healed me so well and it was the faithful prayers of my fellow Christians that the Lord answered so miraculously that I can stand as a living testimony to my almighty God of the universe.

I praise the Lord and thank Him for His mercy and His love for me that is so great that I would be offered a personal Savior in Christ Jesus.

****

TESTIMONY XI

Pastor John Morlan is the son of Pastor Bob and Jann Morlan and the leading pastor of Grace Fellowship Church. His story is a prime example of how God knows us from the moment of our conception, how He works in our lives every moment, even while we are yet sinners, because He has a plan for each of us. God is with every unsaved sinner until death and He is with every born-again Christian for eternity. Pastor John's story is Pastor Bob's and Jann's story, but told from the son's side. God walked with all three of these people—even Bob Morlan while he was still an atheist—even with Jann Morlan as a non-practicing young Catholic, even John Morlan as an unnamed and unborn child in his mother's womb.

The story—as it has been related to me—started out very sadly. It is much more real and much more painful than those stories you receive in your emails—those stories that seem a little hard to believe; one of the forwards your Aunt Mathilda sends to you along with fifteen chain emails that say you'll have bad luck for a year if you don't pass them on. This story is very real—and very sad.

The traumatic events began in January of 1968. Less than two years into their marriage, this couple experienced their first miscarriage. This was the first of a string of two miscarriages and two highly distressing stillbirths. Four children that this young couple hoped would arrive into their world alive and vibrant would tragically not make it into their lives. The two stillborn children are buried not far away in Joliet. Nothing can fill a young couple's lives with confusion and despair like the hopes of four lives cut short before they can joyfully burst upon the scene.

This is the painful backdrop—the tender canvas upon which the whole of their story is painted. Unable to have children naturally, an extraordinary amount of sorrow formed a huge unmet set of needs inside them—especially the sad mother.

At this point in their religious lives, both experienced the events that unfolded upon them from very opposite viewpoints. She was raised as a devout Catholic, though the most recent years' attendance would not have revealed it. He spent his elementary years in and out of a more southern evangelical church setting, though he walked the earth in those days as an atheist. You could probably not envision a greater difference in how two people could view a similar set of circumstances. This difference in worldview added to an already challenging sea of questions, doubts, bitterness, emptiness, and hopelessness that they were already navigating.

Oddly though, these two opposite worldviews would create similar responses from both of them. The would-be mother, a non-practicing Catholic in her 20s, and the would-be father, an outwardly successful business-owning atheist, would both hunger for a healing from those painful losses. Pain still feels real even for people who don't honestly think they have an eternal soul. Both hurt deep down.

A short while later, following the last stillbirth, a new opportunity became available for them to pursue. Adoption! If they adopted a baby, they would have a child to call their own. Maybe it would feel the same as having their own son or daughter; or maybe it wouldn't. They didn't really know. But that didn't stop them from trying.

In June of 1971, more than three years after their first of four babies would die, news came to them from the attorney who had been doing the research for them. An eighteen-year-old from Lockport had become pregnant. Her inability to care for the child because of age and circumstances had concerned her and her parents enough that they decided to pursue adoption. The lawyer notified the young couple, they agreed to move forward, and the following weeks were filled with anticipation.

It wasn't a particularly memorable day, cold, but not anything special one way or the other. It was December 13, 1971. Nothing particularly spectacular happened that day in the world, yet you wouldn't have thought it was a normal day in the New Lenox home of this couple. The excitement began to crescendo when their attorney called on December 13.

The pain of losing those four other children was shoved to the back now—a hospital-blanket-clad son was wrapped in their arms. The memories of the last four years of sorrow were transforming from an everyday struggle to just what I called it—memories. Hope began to spring up again. Hope—that's a strange concept for an atheist, isn't it?

On December 15, 1971, only hours before they would hold their new son for the first time, the phone rang in the father's business office. "We've got some problems," the voice said. "The mother is thinking about keeping the baby."

The lawyer pointed out how the mother was starting to waver on her decision—instant despair! The emotions and memory of losing those two stillborn babies came rushing back like a tidal wave. How on earth was he going to reveal this news to his wife? She had been torn up by all the other horrible disappointments. She was so emotionally beat up by her losses; he didn't think she could take it.

He sat in his office, in that late afternoon moment, and thought a while about what he could do—nothing! He could do absolutely nothing. Not only was he powerless over the course of events, but he knew this news would send his wife into a fresh spiral of despair.

He could do nothing but sit and ponder; wrestling with his soul, and he could talk ... to ... God.

He said, "God, I don't really think You're there. You know I don't believe in You, but if You really exist, and You give us this baby boy, I'll take him to church every week."

What an odd deal to make, especially for someone who didn't even believe in a God a month ago. Especially for someone who didn't even know what it meant to keep a promise of going to church, a place whose doors he didn't darken except for people being carried, married, or buried.

Someone—I think we all know who—answered that atheist's prayer. They got the boy.

On a very snowy December 17, 1971, a baby arrived safely in the arms of two people whose hearts had only begun to heal. Keeping his promise, that dad brought the boy to church—and would continue for four years to attend church with his son—only to find the things he kept hearing a little off-center. For four years that atheist and lapsed Catholic sat in a Christian church and didn't believe in much more than the pews they were occupying. But they kept going. They kept a commitment made by a desperate atheist in the wee hours of possibility.

This story of adoption moves into 1976, where we discover the real reason God opened the doors for this couple: because He wanted to adopt them into His family. During that year, both of them responded to the message of a Father who would send His only Son to die to make the very people who would crucify Him ... equal heirs with the crucified and risen Son. In 1976, those people became Christians by way of a decision of faith.

In some strange way, this adoption has led to many people coming to faith and being adopted into the family of God. How? Those parents? Bob and Jann Morlan, the founding pastor and his wife. Their child? Yours truly, John Morlan. Without God revealing His heart of adoption over three decades ago, many would have never wrestled with God's love. I, too, would go on to come to faith at the age of six.

Having acquired the basic points of knowledge: that I am a sinner, that Jesus is a perfect substitute and sacrifice, and to top it off, that Jesus rose from the dead to show supernatural power over the curse of sin and the stranglehold of death, as a first-grader, I accepted Jesus as my Savior.

****

TESTIMONY XII

The following is a testimony from two people who are truly God's own. I know they will hold a very special place in heaven with God, because their love for Him and their faith in Him are immeasurable.

I did not interview them personally for this book, although it would have been my greatest honor. I can offer the assurance that anyone who knows them will testify that these two people know the Lord beyond any shadow of a doubt.

I know him as Pastor Scott Willis and his wonderful wife Janet. His full name is Duane Scott Willis. Their story of the Lord walking with them and how they continuously bless the Lord in all things is the most astonishing story of faith that has ever been written since Job in the Old Testament of the Bible.

Pastor Scott Willis and his wife Janet had nine children whom they dearly loved and nurtured. In the late morning of November 8, 1994, they lost their six youngest ones in a fiery accident on I-94 on the outskirts of Milwaukee. The news was headlines all over the country in hours and just about every American suddenly knew the Willis name. Only a few hours after the accident, the world learned that Scott and Janet would recover from the second and third degree burns they suffered while trying to rescue their children. The world also learned of the tragic death of the six young children who were suddenly taken from Scott and Janet in a terrible, freak accident.

About a week after the accident, the world was held in total amazement as this couple told everyone how they could make it through all that happened to them that fateful day. Only four months after the accident, I would hear their testimony first hand.

The following is Pastor Scott's and his wife Janet's own words from an audio recording I made of their visit to Grace Fellowship Church as special speakers during an evening service on March 12, 1995, only four months after the terrible accident.

Scott: As we were driving over, Janet said, "You know, it's going to be kind of emotional."

It's been kind of a roller coaster for the last couple of weeks for us, the last three weeks, because we never know how we're going to feel, especially when we get up to talk.

Jan and I were driving up to Milwaukee on November 8, 1994 with our six little ones. We had a great morning.

We had gotten up early. I had to get up at five to open the doors for the voting booth people to place in our church building and the kids had a once-a-week paper route, Penny Saver, that they would do. They would work in pairs. So they had gone out and come back and Janet said they were giving high fives. They were having a really good time that morning, which wasn't usually the case when they had to go to work. We were really thrilled with that. We were happy to see that it seemed that God was working in and among the little ones there. We all piled into the car and headed off toward Watertown, Wisconsin, taking 94, 294 and then back on 94 and then cutting into 894 in Milwaukee.

As we were driving, a little yellow car was in front of me and it just did a little swerve and there was something on the road. I looked and I didn't have time to check my left to see if there was a car over there and I couldn't just pull over and it looked like I might be able to avoid the piece of metal that was in the road. It looked like a binder that was off the back of a truck. There had been a truck in front of the yellow car. It wasn't from that truck, but I thought maybe it had fallen off. I knew my catalytic converter seemed to hang down kind of low on the right, so I basically went right over the center with the car, thinking it might not even hit it, and the next thing I knew the car was jolted sideways into the next lane and I remember just crouching down with the steering wheel to bring the car back out of the slide and all of a sudden around me were flames over the top and around the sides and I just began to yell "Get out of the car, get out of the car!" I was able to get the car out of the slide and get it set down on the side of the road. I reached for the door handle and realized that I was buckled up. I reached down to unsnap my seat belt and there were flames roaring in between the front bucket seats. I remember a thought going through my mind, *"Scott, if you don't put your hand down there and get that seat belt unbuckled you're going to die."*

So I put my hands down in there, unbuckled the seat belt, and finally got the door open and just sort of fell out. There was a concrete bunker there and I fell over that and the next thing I realized I was looking at the van and cars around us had stopped. People had gotten out and one man began to beat on the windows of the van. I went over there, my hands were burned, and I began to use my elbows and my feet to try to kick the windows. We had darkened windows, but not so darkened that you couldn't see in there. You couldn't see through it, but it was all dark. I thank God that I couldn't look in there and see what was in there.

And the next thing I knew I heard Janet going, "No! No! No! No!"

There was a grassy area between the lanes, between the north bound and the south bound, and she was crying out, "No! No! No!"

I remember going over to Janet and I grabbed her by the shoulders and said, "Janet, they're with the Lord! They're with the Lord, and Janet, God has prepared us for this."

I didn't think about saying either of those things; particularly, "God has prepared us for this," but indeed God had and I'd like to share with you tonight how God had prepared us for that and for this as the weeks and months go by. So I'd like to ask you to bow your heads with me and have a word of prayer.

Father, we thank You Lord, for this chance to gather together tonight and Lord, we just want to praise You and thank You for Your goodness and Lord, for Your grace. Thank You for all the things we've learned in the past that came to fruition on that day. Thank You, Lord, for all the people You sent to be a help to us and an encouragement and, Lord, including these folks here tonight. Lord, we want to honor You. We want to give praise to our Savior, the Lord Jesus Christ, so we ask that the Spirit of God would have freedom to work in our hearts, in my heart, and in each heart here, Lord, that Jesus might be magnified. We want to tell You we love You. We ask this in Jesus' name. Amen.

God had prepared us for this. I'm going to have Janet come up and share some things in a little bit. I really don't look at this as a sermon. I just want to share a testimony of what happened.

I was twenty-seven years old. We were living in Sugar Grove, Illinois, and I was teaching at Batavia Junior High School. I was coaching wrestling and we had three little ones and things were going well. As far as paying our bills, we had bought our first house.

Janet was invited to go to a Bible study at a church out in Somonauk. Actually, a girlfriend had been invited by another girlfriend and so Janet's girlfriend invited her to come along as shotgun so that these Baptists weren't going do something with her when they got her over there—try to convert her or something. She went to the Bible study for a few weeks and I remember her coming home and telling me, "Scott, they visit from that church," and I told her that I didn't want anybody coming over and visiting me.

So one Sunday we finally decided to go over there. It was about thirty minutes away. We got in the car, put the three kids in. We went over there and it was culture shock. There were two things that I remember so well on that first Sunday.

I had never been in a Baptist church and so it was a shock. I had gone to church almost all of my life. I had married a Catholic girl and basically we were out of church at this time. We had just kind of drifted away. But I had been faithful in church as a teenager. I was in the youth group, but that Sunday I saw something happen in the church I had never seen before. One was that there was a quartet singing. The guys had lavender suits and the gals had flowered lavender dresses and I was just sitting there with a big grin like I don't believe this. But the thing that was most important was when the preacher got up, he opened the Word of God and he preached from it. I had been in church all of my life. I had never seen anybody preach out of the Bible. I don't remember what he said, I know he preached the gospel, but it went right over my head. I was just sort of in shock.

We were driving away and Janet asked, "What did you think?"
I said, "What did you think?"
She said, "No. What did you think? I asked you first."
I said, "We're never coming back here."

And that went on. I was teaching school and so Thursday I came home from school and Janet had come home from the Bible study and she said, "Scott, there's a couple of men coming from the church."

When I share that, she always wants me to make sure you know that she told them that I said not for anybody to come over. That she wasn't disobedient. They said, "We're coming anyway."

When I came home, she told me there would be men coming and the Spirit of God had prepared my heart so much that I was looking forward to those men coming. I didn't know what they were going to say, but God had prepared my heart.

They came that night and I invited them in. We began talking about the pictures on the wall and about the kids and in my heart I'm thinking this is not why they're here. Yet, I had no idea what the gospel was, so I had no idea what they were there for, but that thought went through my heart that they are not here for that.

A little while later, David Barton took his New Testament out of his pocket and said, "Scott, I'd like you to read some verses." He had asked me, "If you die tonight, would you go to heaven?"

I don't remember, today, what I had said, but I know when David pulled out his Bible. He was the assistant pastor and he shared some Bible verses. He had me read them. One of the verses was: "For all have sinned and come short of the glory of God" (Romans 3:23).

I don't know why, I was one of those types of guys who was always moving around fast, singing in the hallways. It seemed like everything was good on the outside. I would look across the street and it seemed like we had things more together than they did. But the Word of God just stopped me in my tracks.

For all have sinned and come short of the glory of God.

I knew in my heart. I knew indeed that Scott Willis was a sinner. I knew the thoughts I had and the things I would have done had not the law prevented it. I just knew the Word of God was right. I was a sinner. I was lost and on my way to hell. In my living room that night, I got down on my knees and I asked Jesus Christ to be my Savior. I trusted the Lord that night and God saved me. It has been twenty years since that time. It was February the sixth of 1975 that I trusted the Lord as my Savior and God began to teach us. That was the first preparation God had for my life.

Janet had been saved as a teenager. Somebody had handed her a gospel tract and her mom chased the two guys off who gave it to her. We think they were from Moody Bible Institute. We're not sure. But her mom chased them off, being a good Catholic family and Janet didn't know any better. She still had it, went up and read that tract, and prayed that night to accept the Lord as her Savior. But she wasn't in a Bible teaching church and what happened was that she didn't grow and we are not really sure at what point it was, but she had heard a sermon while we were in college. We were married between our sophomore and junior years at Illinois State and she heard a preacher on television talk about salvation. He said if you trust in Christ, then stand up and she stood up. Then he said tell the first person that you see.

Well, I came through the door and I'm as lost as can be and she says, "Scott, I want to tell you that I'm saved and I made Jesus my Savior."

I said, "Oh. Okay." I just let it go right on by me. It had no effect on me at that time. But you know, about seven years later I trusted Christ as Savior and God had prepared us in different ways—but that was the beginning point, when we made Jesus Christ Savior in our lives.

I heard a sermon one time, and it had such a dramatic effect on me. It was taken from Psalm 73 and it is by a man named Asaph and he said, "Truly God is good to Israel, even to such as are of a clean heart" (Psalm 73:1).

The conclusion of the matter is in the very first verse of that psalm. And yet he goes on and says, "But as for me, my feet were almost gone; my steps had well nigh slipped" (Psalm 73:2).

This wasn't a man who came to trust the Lord in sort of a second hand way, like you might pass down an heirloom from one person to another. This is somebody who had experienced the Lord in his life. Asaph went on to say that he looked around and he looked in the garages of his neighbors. The chariots were stacked in there. The corn was in the fields. The kids and the neighbors were healthy. They had no time for God. They wore their pride, he says, around their neck, but they were neck less.

Then he looked at God's people and many of them were hurting. It didn't seem as if the crops were quite as high and there weren't as many chariots in the garage and the kid's noses were running and there were all sorts of troubles.

Then he continues later in that psalm and he says, "Verily I have cleansed my heart in vain, and washed my hands in innocency. For all the day long have I been plagued and chastened every morning. If I say, I will speak thus; behold, I should offend against the generation of thy children" (Psalm 73:13-15).

He was afraid to share how he felt, in that he might lead somebody else astray.

But then he said, "When I thought to know this, it was too painful for me. Until I went into the sanctuary of God; then understood I their end" (Psalm 73:16-17).

Asaph came to a point in his life where he came into the tabernacle of God and realized that life consisted of more than the years upon this earth, that there was an eternity. Asaph realized there was a long view of life. I remember the impact that message had on my life, that one sermon that said Scott, you know there's more than just the days here. In fact, Asaph compares himself to a dog in the sense that he was looking just for today and just for tomorrow, but not looking for eternity.

God began to give Janet and me a view of eternity. God had prepared us for the preaching of other preachers and for teachers and for so many other people. And God had prepared us for that day on November eighth through His Word. If there is anything that has made an impact on us and has given us the comfort, given us the desire to continue, and to have joy in our hearts, it is the Word of God.

I remember seeing a movie about a singer. He was in an airplane crash. He survived, but he was severely burned. He looked like a marshmallow that had been burned a little bit too much. He still sings, but I remember him saying that what was most important to him in getting through those times were the friends that he had. A red flag went up in my mind that it would seem strange to me. I understood the importance of friends, but I knew because of our accident that the thing which was the most comforting and most important to us is the Bible. It gives us the comfort, assurance and the confidence that God is good and that God loves us. God has tenderly secured a place for those children and that we will see them again. It's the Word of God.

We began to read the Bible together all the while in the days after the accident, something we should have done many, many years ago. We were reading in Second Peter and Peter says, "For we have not followed cunningly devised fables, when we made known unto you the power and coming of our Lord Jesus Christ, but were eyewitnesses of his majesty" (2 Peter 1:16).

A lot of people said to us, "God needed your kids for His garden in heaven."

And many, many people talked about our little kids as angels in heaven. But you know what? I've got the Word of God and I know that they're not angels and they're not flowers in the garden. God has them as people, and we will see them again and enjoy them for all eternity. We know that some day when their bodies are raised up, that they will have an eternal and incorruptible body. They are not flowers. I thank God we didn't have to hold on by making up some story to be able to soothe ourselves to take the sorrow away, or to comfort us in our sorrow. We have the Word of God to go to.

It has been twenty years since I was saved on that Thursday night and over those twenty years Jan and I have learned many things from God's Word. There's still so much more to learn, but there have been many things we have learned and I can stand up here tonight and say, after examining the evidence of God's Word, like the writer of Proverbs, every word of God is pure. He is a shield to those who put their trust in Him. God indeed, is our shield.

In preparing us, God had given us a love for His Word. God had revealed the Lord Jesus Christ in our life, in our salvation.

The Bible says for He hath made Him; that is, that God the Father has Him the Son; the Son to be slain for us that we might be made the righteousness of God in Him.

But, you know, I knew that. I knew that Jesus came and shed His blood for me. That's why I came to faith, because I knew I was a sinner, I was lost and on my way to hell, but that Jesus died for me and I accepted that. Through the accident I realized also that Jesus understands the pain a parent has who loses a child. In Hebrews chapter four, it says, "For we have not a high priest which cannot be touched with the feeling of our infirmities" (Hebrews 4:15).

The context is basically about the temptation for sin. But the application is that Jesus knows how we feel. He knows the sorrow in a parent's heart. I also came to an understanding, or at least began to understand, more about the Holy Spirit. I remember standing in the pulpit and teaching about the wonderful work of the Holy Spirit in bringing conviction into a person's life using the Word of God to bring a person to faith. And about the sealing ministry of the Holy Spirit that seals us until the day of redemption and about the enabling work to get the grace for each day. But I hadn't really experienced the comfort. The Holy Spirit is called the Comforter in the Word of God, and the tender mercies of the Holy Spirit began to be real in our lives.

When we were standing there in that grassy area what came to our mind, and we believe it was the Spirit of God bringing it into our mind, were the words from Psalm 34, "I will bless the Lord at all times: his praise shall continually be in my mouth. My soul shall make her boast in the Lord: the humble shall hear thereof, and be glad. O magnify the Lord with me, and let us exalt his name together" (Psalm 34:1-3).

I remember preaching that and teaching our people in Chicago; you know that you praise God. I remember a funeral service for a Chicago policeman with a church building filled, and I remember Kathy, his widow, and saying, "Kathy, here's what you do in time of sorrow. You praise God continually. You praise God publicly."

And all of a sudden those things came back to me. There, standing in that grassy area, those were the words that came to me and came to Janet. Janet went into the ambulance saying, "I will bless the Lord at all times."

She made it definite that she was going to do that. I went off in another ambulance with Benny. The Holy Spirit had worked in our lives. God had prepared us through His Word and through the Spirit's work in our life. God had prepared us as well, for what happened in the accident, in the examples of faith.

In the Old Testament there is a person named Joseph, one of Jacob's sons. We named our little Joey after Joseph. Joseph was a man who was betrayed, sold by his brothers, falsely accused when he was in Egypt, ended up in prison, was forgotten about in prison by somebody he had helped, and yet, in God's timing, Joseph had never lost his love and his confidence in God. At the time that God had said, Joseph came out of prison. Joseph was awed—he who had never lost faith in the one true God—and was honored to be reunited with his family. I thank God for that example.

I think of Paul and Silas, in times of trouble, singing and praising God in the jail. Those are things that we were taught, never knowing that in times of trial they were our examples as well.

So many people have said you know that's a Job like experience, but there's so many differences between the story of Job and how he was belittled. People have been nothing but gracious to us and have been so kind and so good to us. Not only people, but the media and everybody has been just unbelievably kind to us. But there's a verse in Job and it says, "He hath loosed my cord and afflicted me" (Job 30:11).

We were reading that aloud and I said, "I don't understand that." So I looked a little bit closer. I had a parallel translation. It says, "He hath unstrung my bow string and afflicted me" (paraphrase), and I began to just weep, because over in Psalm 127 it says we are like archers and our children like arrows that we send out.

"Lo, children are an heritage of the Lord and the fruit of the womb is his reward. As arrows are in the hand of a mighty man; so are children of the youth. Happy is the man that hath his quiver full of them: they shall not be ashamed, but they shall speak with the enemies in the gate" (Psalm 127:3-5).

It seemed to me that God had cut that bowstring. He had taken those children. My quiver was empty. I have three older ones who are grown with their own families, but the quiver at home was empty now. I realized that was self pity; that God had a purpose, even in the short time of Pete's life, six weeks, and Ben, thirteen years. I think of David and his example. David had failed God and I knew I had failed God miserably. There have been times I had just failed God, in my heart, in my actions, and in what I said. David had failed God. He had gone through trials and yet he could say in Psalm 13, "But I have trusted in thy mercy; my heart shall rejoice in thy salvation. I will sing unto the Lord, because he hath dealt bountifully with me" (Psalm 13:5-6).

I remember the heroes and the examples of faith. When I was in college, I had a teacher named Dr. Suell. He taught several of the preaching classes and education classes and I had him for about three or four classes. He was a big, red-haired Texan. His voice was as big as Texas.

His wife was driving their children to school one day. The little one in the front seat, about two years old, reached over and hit the latch on the door and the child began to fall out the door and the mom reached over to grab the boy and as she did she brought the wheel over with her. The boy fell out; the back wheel rolled over him and killed that little boy. I had Dr. Suell for a teacher at that time and I remember when we came back to class, the first class session. Dr. Suell got up in front and began to teach. He must have sensed that all of these guys were sitting on the edge of their seats. They just didn't know what to think, what to say, and how to react. He just stopped and gave testimony to God's goodness and to the fact he was confident he would see his son again and just gave glory to God. I don't remember his words, but I know they touched my heart such that I've never forgotten it. It had been such a testimony to me—and what an example of faith!

I thank God too; in preparing us in that God had shown us we had a hope, that we have a *sure hope*. The word hope in the Bible is not just like I wish I'm going to get a whole bunch of Christmas presents, but that it is sure. You can make your list, and maybe you will get a couple of them, but when it comes to the Bible, it says it is hope, you can mark it down because it is assured. I *know* Jesus is going to come back, but if He tarries first I know that to be absent from the body is to be present with the Lord. I'll see our children again. Jan and I pray hard that the Lord will come back soon—God, change Your timetable. Make it sooner, so we can see those children.

Jesus said, "I am the resurrection and the life: he that believeth in me, though he were dead yet shall he live: and whosoever liveth and believeth in me shall never die" (John 11:25-26).

I'd like Janet to come up and share an incident that happened when we had gotten back from the hospital.

Janet: My hands had healed somewhat, and I saw a baby card that had been sitting around the house and it was an illustration of a baby on the front and I thought that I would straighten up. It was from Pete when he was six weeks old, and so I went to throw it in the garbage and as I did, I just glanced back and my hand was hanging onto the little foot and I let go and I thought of Pete being buried and it really choked me up. I thought, *"Well, I'll just step around the corner here into the bathroom and have myself a good cry."*

As I got in and shut the door, the Lord brought a verse to my mind, a really, really powerful verse—"Woman, why weepest thou" (John 20:15).

I realized that's what Jesus said to Mary when she was weeping in front of the tomb and He was standing right in front of her—alive. It was like the Lord telling me, *"Janet, Pete is alive just as much as I was, there."*

I quickly dried my eyes and ran out and checked my Bible to make sure I had the right context and it was the resurrection scene. Just then, my brother and sister-in-law walked in the door. I knew they were coming, but I had forgotten and had they walked in then, I would have been in the bathroom, red-eyed and upset. I think the Lord just wanted me calm at that time. Also, it wasn't that He was saying I couldn't weep, but I realized that it's okay to sorrow. We miss the kids and we still cry every day, but we don't sorrow with those who have no hope. That's a totally different type of weeping and He was saying, "Woman, why weepest thou?"

We had been advised to be careful that our sorrow didn't get mixed up with bitterness or self-pity. I think that maybe on that occasion, I was leaning toward self-pity. The Lord's Word has been a comfort, not only in bringing verses to my memory, but as we read His Word, it has been our counsel.

Scott: I also think that God has prepared us in our family, and in the family that He has given to us. I thank God for a faithful wife, with a meek and quiet spirit, who's a hard worker, as wife, mother, and teacher. We homeschooled the kids, so they were always around us, especially around Janet. We have three older children and six grandchildren with two due this summer. So, Lord willing, by the end of summer we'll have eight.

It was so wonderful in how God had helped us. As we see the kids play, there's been a kindred spirit among our kids. Pete was born with five nieces and nephews and Elisabeth had a niece, so our kids just sort of mixed in with the grandkids and they played together. There was a kindred spirit among them and it was such a delight.

When Toby was over with his family or Dan, but Dan didn't have any children, it was sort like I was the grandparent over everyone and the other kids were the parents and then all the little grandkids.

I was in church one day about a year ago. This was before Pete, but Hank was standing by me and we had a homecoming Sunday where people come back once a year and we have kind of a big day. Hank was standing by me, kind of jumping around and a man walked by and said, "Oh! Is that your grandson?"

I said, "No. That's my boy." I didn't tell him there was another one underneath. I don't remember if Jan was pregnant at that time with Elisabeth, but I just kind of kept my mouth shut. It was a humbling experience. I thought for sure he would think this was my son.

One of the wonderful things was that the boys were my boys' heroes. I have a book that I just think so much of, and it's called How to Be a Hero to Your Kids, by Josh McDowel and Dick Day. I think it is a wonderful book. I wasn't my kid's hero; their brothers were their heroes. I take satisfaction in that Toby's closer to me in age than he was to his youngest brother, so I guess that gets me off the hook a little bit. But when they talk of heroes, I think of Ryan Sandberg and Frank Thomas and so on, but they talk of their big brother, Toby.

He had been a wrestling state champ. He would come home every weekend at our church and he took time with the kids and Dan, when he would come home, he was six years up in Watertown. He lives up there and whenever we saw him, he worked all summer at wrestling camp, so he was gone from home most of the time, but when he was home he took the time with the kids and he would organize games, he would tell them camp stories as they were going to bed at night and what a blessing! When I think back on the kids I think, what a blessing that there was a kindred spirit between the older three and the little ones and the grandkids. We've asked God for a special love for our grandkids. You know, it's hard being a parent of younger kids than your grandkids. It's hard to dote on your grandkids. We've asked God to give us that doting spirit on our grandkids, and on our church kids, and on our neighborhood kids.

Our boys loved baseball. One of the hardest things was when Christmas time came. We had a lot of media call back and they wanted to do something for television and newspapers. We gave a couple of interviews, one on TV and one on the radio and one newspaper.

The question that came up was, "What about Christmas? How are you going to manage Christmas?"

Janet had to admit she and Elisabeth had started to prepare the Christmas things early in November. Janet would tell Elisabeth how we were going to decorate the tree and all of that, but you know, the heart was kind of taken away of wanting to decorate and put up a tree and put out the little lights and the little toys and so on. Then she began thinking and realized that if it wasn't for Christmas there would be no cross and without the cross there would be no resurrection hope and so we got out the Christmas things.

Christmas is always kind of hectic with all the family. It's going to be tough.

In a month I'll be helping out in little league—my boys aren't going to be out there. They loved baseball, all four of them. They just loved it and it was a joy to my heart to help out on the one team of the two boys. And God kind of closed some things for us. Hank was only six. Sam's team, which was a seven, eight, nine team, needed a player.

They were one player short, so they asked the kids did anybody have a little brother and Sam said, "I do." So Hank got to play.

It was the second game of the year and they got the game going. He made two plays. He never really bent down and got hit in the face with a ground ball, so he just stuck the old mitt down there, caught it and did what he had to do. I was watching Ben and Joe playing the game and then a little while later I looked behind me in the fence and it's Hank. Hank and Sam were playing another game at another field. I said, "Hank, what are you doing?"

He said, "Dad! Dad! I got to pitch! I got to pitch!"

He had been begging the coach all year. He's only six years old. I found out that the next inning had started and Hank was supposed to pitch a second inning too, and here Hank was over there talking to me and everybody was looking around trying to find out where Hank is. He made it back in time. He got to pitch two innings. He only pitched two innings that year, but he was the only pitcher who didn't give up a run all year. When he got out there to pitch, he must have been watching some cartoons because he'd get out there and he'd wind the old arm up and let 'er fly, and he said the coaches didn't know what to do so they just let him do it. So we just called it the Bugs Bunny windup and he got through two innings that way. So that kind of helped to close some things up for us.

Now I'll get into the next thing of how God has prepared us. He has given us some wonderful memories. When I pastored here, Ben Peterson had come, who had been an Olympic wrestler, a gold medal winner. We had invited him to our church in Chicago several years later for a father-son and also to speak. I remember Ben speaking on building memories in your family.

God has prepared us for this in that we look back and God has given us a whole bunch of wonderful memories. My mother and father-in-law used to go around with that video camera and I'd go, "Aw, here they are."

I praise God for them and that they did that. We've now got video tapes of our kids and I'll just go over and I'll put one of them in and I'll get to see Joe pitch again. I see Sam's first big hit. He reaches up over his head and laces one into left field and when he gets to second base the camera focuses in and it's priceless to see the smile on his face.

Our six children were Ben, being Ben, Benjamin because he was the child of our old age. That's what it says about Jacob's son Benjamin; child of his old age. There's a ten-year difference between our third and our fourth. Ben was a chivalrous, creative kid. He was more of the arts kind. He loved to draw, to paint, loved King Arthur and reading and all those adventurous things. None of our kids had made that step and although Ben was thirteen and he had began to change in his looks and you could see that he was becoming a young man. He was small. He was scrawny, but he wanted to be a hero.

One day he and Hank were sword fighting. We did things like that around our house. Hank was getting better than Ben and Hank was only six and Ben was thirteen and probably (they) were six and twelve at the time.

I remember calling Ben over and putting my arm around him and saying, "Ben, do you really think you could have been a knight?"

He just gave me that jaw and said, "Yes I do!"

But when the accident happened, Benny was sitting in the middle seat, he and Pete. The four little ones were in the back. The gas tank had exploded. There was a hole in the floorboard in the back and the floor of the back had been for sleeping. They probably died instantaneously. They probably never knew what happened and probably Peter either, but Ben had to have unbuckled his seatbelt, found the latch for the lock, then found the other latch for the door to open up. Our locks automatically opened in the front when you pull the handle, but Ben's didn't. Janet had been sleeping reclined in her seat so maybe Ben had to work around that, but you know, when Ben made it out, we didn't think anybody was out. It wasn't until like a minute or thirty seconds later that we realized Ben had made it out. But I thought, *"Boy what courage for a little kid to be able to unbuckle his seatbelt, get that lock, and open the door."* He was in the rage of where the fire was and his clothes were basically burned off except around his waist. The fire underneath had burned his shoes and his face was all burnt. I thought, and this is a thought only a dad would have, I thought, *"Benny, you'd have been a knight."*

We Never Walk Alone

After Ben came, Joe came. We didn't want Ben to be alone so we kind of hoped we'd have another one. Joseph is also called child of my old age, so we had these two children in our old age.

Joe was intense. He was our loose cannon. Joe was two steps ahead of us, probably the smartest of the group. He loved athletics, loved baseball. He was a southpaw. Benny, Joe, and Elisabeth were all lefties. Joe had just a burning passion to play ball. He was very competitive and sometimes we had to put the lid on him.

When we talk about the kids, people say, "Well, there's six children." And they might see a video tape on the TV and know what they look like, but you know who they are? They're our kids, they are the ones who we rubbed their heads, we pinched them, and tickled them, and laughed with them. I remember Joe took so many spankings. That poor boy, he got more spankings than the rest of them combined. We kind of laugh a little bit as we cry about it and think that Joe's not going to get any more spankings.

Sammy was our sixth and probably the most spiritual of all the kids. He was so different from the others. He was blonde and big shouldered and while all the other guys were kind of scrawny, Sam was big boned and we called him our California boy. Sam, though we called him Sambo, read through a beginner's Bible three times. He just loved reading it. He liked to draw, he loved sports, but he wasn't old enough to settle into any particular favorites. He tried everything that Ben and Joe did. He was a really likeable little kid. And then Hank came along and Hank was probably the one who was the closest to me. He was my Boston boy.

When Janet was pregnant with Hank, we didn't know if it was going to be a boy or a girl, but we were talking about names and one day I came home I said, "Janet, I got it. If it's a boy, it'll be Hank Boston!"

She looked at me and knew I was telling the truth; that that's what it was going to be. Hank was named after the husband, and my good friend, of the lady who had invited Janet to the Bible study.

So he was named after Hank; Boston came because since the nineteen fifties I was a Ted Williams fan and he played for the Boston Red Sox, so I had become a Red Sox fan. So here is the kid and all of our other kids have some Bible name in there somewhere, the first three just by luck and the other ones because we determined it. So here comes Hank Boston. He too had read through the beginner's Bible that Sam had. He never walked; he jumped. He was just full of so much life. We were looking at the video tape they had shown on TV of him and he was just over there and just in constant motion, a happy-go-lucky kid who was always smiling.

Then when we thought we were going to have another boy, our hearts were just figuring on another boy, and we got Elisabeth. What a joy that was. You would think with four older brothers at home she would be a tomboy, but it was just the opposite. She was just like her momma. She was so skinny and so fragile and so precious and she'd come in and she would pirouette around in the room. It was just a blessing to see her and to snuggle with her. She was just so much like Janet that Janet said she could read her mind. Janet would get something out to sew and Elisabeth would be on the other side moving the bolt of material down or getting ingredients to make something. She just seemed to know what Janet wanted. She was a momma's girl. She wasn't a daddy's girl; she was a momma's girl. I'd come in saying, "Where's my pumpkin girl?" and she'd hide behind Janet's skirts. She really was a momma's girl.

Then Pete was our last. Pete was wide-eyed when he was born. He was our smallest and his eyes barely looked out. He looked like a little puppy. But after six weeks his eyes were big and the night before, Toby called up and said, "Hey, I'd like to come over and play some football with the boys."

So he jogged a couple of miles from his house, played football; his wife, Brenda, and their little ones came over and played with Elisabeth and Jan and I took Pete to the mall with all the decorations there in early November, getting ready for Christmas. You'd think that the little guy would be looking around, but the whole time he just scrunched around and just looked at us the whole time and we thought boy, that was kind of funny. We look back and it seemed that God just kind of closed things up for us. Pete had a little cleft in his chin like his pop.

We were a crazy family. I like to say we were unorthodox in everything except doctrine. We would have gunfights in the OK corral. Toby would come over and he would bring Nerf dart guns and the next thing you know we would be having shoot outs. If the people only knew what was happening up in the church building where we lived in the church. I remember going to camp the first year that we went to family camp and somehow or other our Ben was into Spiderman and they had taken the kids on off to play. Then about lunch time, after the parents had their session and the kids came back for lunch, Ben came over and on his little name tag it said Peter Parker. He had conned those counselors into thinking his name really was Peter Parker and then probably thought he was. Those who knew Ben, in his imagination, he probably thought he was, because Peter Parker was Spiderman's real name. Spiderman, I suppose, is just as real. But there were a lot of crazy things. I think of the time when I came home and there was a hole in my office window from the parking lot. I was walking up the stairs and there's a long-faced Hank and right next to the window there was a brick area where the name of the church and the cross hangs down. Hank was practicing pitching and put one right through the window in the office. You know, I couldn't even get mad. I just had to laugh about it. That wasn't normally me but, it's a lot of great memories.

Through all of it, there were lessons to learn and I would like to briefly share some of those lessons.

The first thing is that salvation is of the Lord, neither is our salvation in any other name given among men under heaven whereby we must be saved. That was the preaching of the apostles in the new church after Christ went back into heaven. No salvation in any other than Jesus Christ. I thank God for sending those men; for David Barton opening up the Bible and sharing with me how I could know that my sins were forgiven; how I could have the peace in my heart that passeth all understanding, to know for sure that if I were to die this day, I would go to heaven.

But you know, I also thank God for His salvation because my four older boys had all made the decision for the Lord. What a joy for me as three weeks before the accident, I was standing in the baptism tank with Hank and I could say, "On your profession of faith, my brother, I baptize you."

Hank was truly my brother in the Lord and what a joy having that and knowing that. We know that some day we are going to see them again because they knew the Lord Jesus Christ as Savior. The best we know, we have confidence they truly understood they were sinners and that Jesus died for them. Even a child—Elisabeth was three and a half; Peter was six weeks—and we knew they wouldn't be able to understand that. We know God is a gracious and a good God. David, when he lost his infant son said, "Can I bring him back again? I shall go to him, but he cannot come back to me." David knew he would see his son again and I thank God for His gracious hand for little ones. And we have confidence, all the confidence, 100 percent confidence that we will see our children again. I thank God for His salvation.

Another lesson we understood as we look back is that death, the whole idea of death, is changed for us. There is no fear of death. About two years ago, I looked at myself in the mirror. I didn't look too much different than I do now because I had put back on some of that weight and I said, "You know something Scott? You are going to die if you don't get yourself straightened out and get exercising."

So I joined the Chicago Health Club and began to work out and get the cardio-vascular thing so I would be healthy. I had a brother who died about three years ago of a heart attack. He was forty-nine. My dad died of heart disease and I was getting worried about my situation. But then I looked at the Word of God and it says in First Corinthians fifteen, "O death, where is thy sting? O grave, where is thy victory? The sting of death is sin; and the strength of sin is the law. But thanks be to God, which giveth us the victory through our Lord Jesus Christ. Therefore my beloved brothers be steadfast, unmovable, always abounding in the work of the Lord forasmuch as ye know that your labour is not in vain in the Lord" (1 Corinthians 15:55-58).

I realized, before the accident, that Jesus had died and risen and He had conquered death and the grave, but you know, it came home to me because all of a sudden I realized I had that same sure hope, because the Lord arose so I too, being a believer in Jesus Christ, would be able to pass from this earth into eternity, into heaven and be with the Lord. And Janet and I, every night we say, "God, thank You for a day that's gone by. Thank You for one day closer to seeing Jesus face to face and thanking Him and also for seeing our kids."

We get up in the morning and we thank God for another day to serve Him and we say God, may we serve You with a joy and with an excitement for the day that You've given to us.

God changed that idea about death. Death for the Christian is life eternal and being reunited with our loved ones.

Our third lesson was how precious time is with our kids. I know there was something on television I had said up in Milwaukee at a meeting and it is so true and that is: there are regrets in my heart. I don't think anybody probably could ever say there are no regrets. I wish I could do two things. I wish I could get them back for one minute and say Joe, it doesn't matter if you strike out four times. Joe I love you. It doesn't matter whether you drop the ball. No matter what, I love you unconditionally. I know they knew that, but you know from a dad's heart I wish I could tell them that again. And there is one other thing I have a regret about—that there were so many times that they said, "Dad I want to tell you something, I want to tell you what happened," or "Will you listen to me read this story?" or "Dad I want to show you something" or "Dad, will you help me on this?" and I'd say, "You know, I don't have time right now" or "This is a good football game" or "I'm watching a movie guys. I'll try to get to you in a little bit." I'll tell you what. If I had a chance again, I'd say, "OK guys, here I am. My ears are bent toward you. I just want to sit here and listen to you." When I get to heaven I just know they are going to want to tell me about all they have experienced from November eighth to whenever I see them and I just want to sit down and say, "OK guys, I'm going to listen. We have all of eternity and I am ready to listen." But you know? I regret as I look back that I lost a lot of time on things that weren't very important, things that had no eternal value and things that didn't affect the lives of my children like they ought to. I urge parents with children to understand that time is so precious and you don't know how much time you have with them. We never thought we were training our children up to be little Samuels, to love and serve God from their time of birth. We would pray right after they were born and dedicate them to the Lord. We felt they would grow up and whatever job they would do, they would do it with a heart of love for God and that they would be a testimony for the Lord Jesus, whether as a carpenter or a school teacher or a preacher or missionary or a housewife or whatever. We never realized the shortness of time.

Janet, would you come up and share about your gratefulness?

Janet: We want to be sure and say how unbelievably grateful we are to everyone for their prayers. We've gotten so many cards and letters and I'm still on the catch up and the backlog reading them and they are even more precious now and I just want to say thank you. At one point it occurred to us that maybe we were the most prayed for people in the world for a while there and we are just very, very grateful to you all.

Scott: We're thankful to realize that God uses people. All our bills are paid, the funeral expenses, the medical bills, all more than enough.

The fourth thing we realized is that we were prepared in a sense and I would like to encourage you to ask the question of yourself: are you prepared? If something were to happen, whether you were to have to, this very night, face the Lord; if death were to come and you were to face the Lord, would you be prepared? Would you be ready? Do you know the Lord Jesus Christ as Savior?

I thank God for all the preachers, all the teachers, all the Christian friends, books we have read, conversations, and examples of other Christians and just for so many things that people have done to teach us we might come to love the Lord more. And in that preparation, God has used so many people and so many things. It is so easy to go to church and to leave church and never listen.

I remember when soon after I was first saved, I was a college graduate. I figured, "Hey I'll watch this guy's grammar and I'll see whether he has things in parallel construction and all that." Then I remembered a little preacher preaching and he said, "You can come to a message with a critical spirit but God has a blessing if it's from the Word of God." It just changed my thinking all around. I've heard what I consider to be bad sermons and I got a blessing from them because I was looking for the blessing in there. God had prepared us. We had taken time to read God's Word. We had taken time for devotions. We weren't really faithful all of the time. There were times we stumbled, but I thank God for the time spent in His Word. There are so many people who go through life and so many Christians who go through troubles and never read God's Word and then when the time of reckoning comes for them they are not prepared. They don't have the depth to be able to deal with the truth of God's Word. They don't have confidence that God is good and has a reason for all things.

Lastly, I learned a lesson that God had gotten my attention and I needed to take a serious look at my life. The preacher will be able to say we can prepare a message and not prepare our heart; I was guilty of that. Many, many times I had stepped to the pulpit. I had prepared a message, but I had not prepared my heart. I ask God to prune the good for the better, that God would teach me through this so many things, that there would be changes in my life, in my thought life, in the things that I do and the things that I say.

Let me close with one thing. We had a reporter come to our house and they videotaped it for Channel 32. It never went on the news. But he asked an interesting question. "What's the mustard seed in all this?"

I suppose the man was a Christian or at least had Bible training. The mustard seed, that smallest seed—if we have the faith of a mustard seed—he asked, "What's the mustard seed in all this?"

Let me share what the mustard seed is, what the real core is in all of this.

Jan and I are ordinary people. Those who know us know that. They know we are not flashy. There is nothing uniquely special about us. We are regular people, but God's grace is available to us and to each one of you. If you don't know that if you died tonight, you would go to heaven, God's grace is available. God will save you.

"For by grace are ye saved through faith; and that not of yourselves: it is the gift of God: Not of works, lest any man should boast" (Ephesians 2:8-9).

The grace for salvation God gave us is available to anyone, as is the grace to carry on, the grace to endure whatever comes our way. God will give the grace so He might be glorified. If you are not saved, the most important thing in all the world is to be prepared to meet God and to have a relationship with Jesus Christ. But it doesn't stop there. That's only the beginning of the preparation. It's to come to know Jesus Christ and we come to do that through reading God's Word, through prayer, and through fellowship with other Christians. We encourage you parents to take time to realize the preciousness of that time. Also, I don't believe the accident happened as a punishment for us, but I realized it was a time to look at my life.

Maybe you need to take a look at the status of your life in terms of serving God and having the right heart's attitude.

✻✻

EPILOGUE

You have read twelve testimonies from twelve people. These people have this in common: they all discovered that God was with them all of their lives and He was working in their lives for the sole purpose of drawing each one of them to Him. They also decided to take the road to salvation and, having done that, they each now know they have God's assurance of eternal life in heaven with Him.

To take the road to salvation you need only to do the following. First, you must pray to God and in this prayer you must acknowledge to God the fact that you are a sinner.

> For it is written, There is none righteous, no, not one. (Romans 3:10)

> For all have sinned, and come short of the glory of God. (Romans 3:23)

Secondly, you must acknowledge that you are lost in your sin and condemned to hell for it.

> For the wages of sin is death; but the gift of God is eternal life through Jesus Christ our Lord. (Romans 6:23)

Thirdly, you need to know that Jesus Christ died as a pure sacrifice for the atonement of your sin and that He arose three days after His crucifixion to heaven and sits at the right hand of God. Knowing this, you must tell God you now accept His Son, Jesus Christ, as your personal Savior.

> That if thou shalt confess with thy mouth the Lord Jesus, and shalt believe in thine heart that God hath raised him from the dead, thou shalt be saved.
> For with the heart man believeth unto righteousness; and with the mouth confession is made unto salvation. (Romans 10:9-10)

> For whosoever shall call upon the name of the Lord shall be saved. (Romans 10:13)

Lastly, you need the faith to know that it is only by God's grace through the sacrifice of His Son's life that you can be saved. There is nothing you can do to earn your way to heaven.

> For by grace are ye saved through faith; and that not of yourselves: it is the gift of God: Not of works, lest any man should boast. (Ephesians 2:8-9)

If you have done these things, you are now a child of God. I welcome you to the family of God.

I encourage you to find a church which preaches and believes all you have learned so you can begin to grow in Christ and be baptized as a profession of your faith in Him. You need to do this because it is important for you to fellowship with other believers and to learn from all of the Scriptures so you can find your gifts and talents that God has given you so that you can go out to the world and share the good news with the world.

Do this so that one day you will mature into a man or woman of God.

Printed in the United States
50007LVS00004B/40-57